Dedicated to the memory of David Bainbridge
1941—2013

The editors would like to thank all the contributors
to this book.

Published by Underwing Press.
www.underwingpress.com

ISBN 978-0-9928185-0-0

The views expressed in this publication are not necessarily those of the Editors.

Designed by Dan Russell and Textbook Studio.

Cover photos: Details from *Tongues of Stone*, 2011. Created by Dorita Hannah,
Carol Brown and Russel Scoones for STRUT. Photos by Christophe Canato.

Proof Reader Ruth Allan.

Contents

Introduction

— Jane Calow

This volume is a collection of specially written pieces combined with images that trace developmental paths in current interdisciplinary arts practices. Specific historical perspectives and contexts are addressed throughout, with analysis and reflection, offering intimations of emergent practices. Reaction to changes in cultural, economic, political and material social conditions are touched upon. All texts invoke multi-faceted and multifarious voices. Pace within each contribution is balanced carefully, thoughtfully. All are dense, succinct and condensed. Imaging does not figure as 'illustrating' written texts – but is seen as text in its own right. Within the volume, images may constitute documentation, 'sketch' or work in progress, or perhaps evidence of other relations. The imaging within this text is not an 'and' – it is integral to our response as editors to the dialogical nature of projects in interdisciplinarity.

At the time of writing: seeking contexts

It is a matter of weeks since the death and funeral of former UK Prime Minister Margaret Thatcher. From taking office in 1979 the ideologically driven divisiveness perpetrated by her leadership furthered fragmentation between and within communities, the repercussions of which are still palpable and painful today. For Thatcher (despite contemporary contestation over her precise wording) there was no such thing as society, only individuals and families. On the morning of her funeral, current Conservative UK Prime Minister, David Cameron, stated that 'we're all Thatcherites now'[1]. For younger generations that did not live through Thatcher's period of office, her impact upon society must be difficult to grasp. Outpourings in the media about 'her life and times' have been extraordinary; from the reading of her 'official' autobiography on BBC Radio 4 to eulogies on how she 'brought the country together'. There is even a proposal for a museum and library to her memory and 'achievements', modelled on the one to Ronald Reagan. For many artists, social thinkers and activists who lived through this period and found it deeply troubling, this attempt at sliding over conflicts – of re-writing history and its lived social conditions – is alarming. The construction of an/the 'official' version of a history, is potentially both depressing and paradoxically, optimistic. For as Foucault has observed, where there is manifestation of power there are always nodal points of resistance. Can interdisciplinarity, with its implied necessity to attend closely to others within dialogical forums, suggest stratagems that may contribute to the application of nodal pressures? We publish this volume at a point when the Arts in Britain are under ideologically driven siege. Interdisciplinarity may offer the potential for opening up new multi-faceted discursive spaces and practices. Recognising the ghost of Thatcherism is not to look inward, or backward, towards a 'Little Britain'. Thatcherism sits within the global context of New Capitalism and corporateness. Living within the conditions of New Capitalism and encountering new corporateness brings to bear major pressures and preoccupations for and within the shifting structures of societies. It calls for negotiation in a climate of contestation, making the need to discover pathways capable of carrying emergent forms of representation ever more urgent. What comes to mind is the need for action – movement – that recognises the to-and-fro between the global and the local and interchange at the point of lived social process.

Against a mood of insecurity brought about by global crises, in his text *Together: The Rituals, Pleasures and Politics of Cooperation* Richard Sennett sets out with some degree of cautious optimism, the conditions and social benefits of cooperation as a means to oil 'the machinery of getting things done.'[2] The optimism displayed by his text flies in the face of divisiveness, of a climate that may appear as sliding towards helplessness. His focus is upon the application of responsiveness and cooperation in communities and work, noting the ethical character of working sympathetically and listening to others.

For our volume we draw upon what Sennett calls 'dialectic and dialogic conversations'[3]. This book is organised under three main sections, the overarching themes of which grew from a reflective, creative and organic process of discussion – firstly between the editors and then between editors and contributors. All entered into dialogue; part and parcel of good interdisciplinary practice.

Section 1

Pleasure and Fear in Interdisciplinary Arts Practice was borne out of the excitement of working in uncharted waters, the sheer pleasure in latent, incredible, buoying creativity – a 'what if'? But 'what if' carries the capacity of summoning unwanted, uncomfortable experience, bringing about collision over potential drawbacks and their subsequent consequence and outcome.

Within 'old school' Modernist language came the idea of risk-taking. What was inferred was some kind of romanticised, heroic, baring of soul – a directness of expression from artist (he) through (largely) painting, directly to (a) viewer, invoking a phantasised heroic giving up of a self.

Against this trope, within the economic and material climatics of now, fear is another matter. Fear of failure, of being exposed can have real psychic, physical and material consequences if research, if practice, fails to deliver economic rewards or cultural capital.

Our first author Carol Brown describes her practice as taking place at the intersections between movement, architecture and performance. Performance and awareness of viscerality is embedded and embodied, conjured within and through her text. Analytically and in a form of poetics she explores the conditions and desire for engagement, to find oneself, to orient oneself as trespasser in a foreign landscape. Carol Brown calls for the demonstration of sympathy towards and respect for the other – the need to develop and show sensitivity in inter-subjective action and encounter in the act of negotiating the symbolic systems of other disciplinary activities.

In conversation with Laura Mansfield, Brave New Alps (Bianca Elzenbaumer and Fabio Franz) discuss and describe their project Department 21, developed during study for an MA in Communication Art and Design at the Royal College of Art. Department 21 was conceived as a conduit to bring together students from different disciplinary departments, creating a convivial space and place for peer to peer learning, and in so doing challenging institutional frameworks through an exercise in de-territorialisation. Department 21 was devised and put into action at a juncture when the financial costs incurred in education have become ever more burdensome, prompting some students and academics to consider other ways of constructing hubs of exchange and learning. Brave New Alps are calling for the building of communities bound by trust.

For Jane Calow, the text is a lull in the production of her artwork in the making, where the final destination is yet to be discovered. The imaged text explores the articulation of narratives en-knotted with class, work and mourning. Echoing the very form of journeying, migration in language between disciplines is navigated within contexts that touch geology, geography, psychoanalysis, language and epistemology.

Section 2

Section 2 considers potential forays into *Mutuality – Collaboration and Interdisciplinary Arts Practice*. Like interdisciplinarity, the term collaboration is frequently used in artistic, cultural and academic circles with small regard for reflection or analysis; indeed the two terms are often conflated or applied interchangeably. Attending closely to these terms, the three contributors in this section make and deliver unsentimental, analytical responses through consideration and articulation of the conditions of their respective grounded practices.

At the emergence of Performance Studies in the 1970s, Richard Schechner – one of its original voices – embraced 'inter' as a means to oppose the dominance of any single system of knowledge. In his contribution to this volume, Mike Pearson points out how this may lead to a crisis of identity with an attendant danger of appropriation – a danger that has dogged other areas such as cultural studies. Through close readings of projects he draws out the specifics of epistemologies and discourses, tracing out the layers of particular forms and languages; for example, the interpenetration of two disciplines – theatre and archaeology.

In tracking the particular trajectories and histories of his practice as artist, educationalist and curator, Daniel Hinchcliffe teases out some of the conditions that bring about cultural change and exchange. Within ever evolving dynamics of socio-historical, economic and technological change, Daniel Hinchcliffe considers interdisciplinarity in conjunction with specific institutions and sets of practices. He indicates how interdisciplinarity has the potential to challenge a presumed 'natural order of things' against a backdrop of cultures of competition between disciplines, departments and individuals.

In the course of writing about her artwork, *Reception*, Becky Shaw came to question the very notion of collaboration. Situated within the Department of Social and Policy Sciences at the University of Bath, *Reception* offered a means by which boundaries between identities and others could unfold across and between disciplines. The artwork was instrumental in opening up a discursive space, rather than space for a collaborative project. In *Reception*, the artist is positioned as neither inside nor outside the department, rather *Reception* is instrumental in shaping a space that considers the public front of intellectual pursuit at the same time as posing the question: 'what is it to form an individual identity within a context?'

Section 3

Ethics, Interdisciplinary Arts Practice and the Politics of Negotiation. At a time when many arts practices can be deemed to have problematised social and ethical conditions of artistic production to such a degree that art can seem immobilised or just irrelevant, it seems appropriate to think the possibility of a simultaneous 'working through' of ethics and arts practices.

Jane Rendell alerts us to how interdisciplinary arts and humanities practice is in danger of being harnessed to secure neo-liberalist government and market-driven policy. In order to counter these tactical manoeuvres, Rendell suggests attending to the psychic dimension of interdisciplinarity; a dimension that offers insights into the transformational potential and transitional status of interdisciplinarity. Mindful of critical, ethical and political dimensions, the dialectics of exteriority and interiority, of latent potentialities, intra-psychic identifications are offered as a site of potential resistance to appropriation. Appropriation is rendered up as 'multi' rather than 'inter'. Contra to isolations within the 'multi', 'inter/intra' intimates potential, of movement within/between/across psychic, metaphorical and physical spatialisation.

Interdisciplinary arts, activism and research organisation Platform present an imperative – a commitment to countering the mechanics of neutralization and shaping of cultural representation deployed by global corporations – in particular, international oil companies. In considering the artistic practice and environmental thrust of Platform's work, Jane Trowell (a member of Platform) draws attention to how global corporations appropriate the arts as vehicles to provide veils of social legitimacy. She describes how international companies can attempt to present a face of false liberality through sponsorship and money for the arts. Her text highlights the relationship between the Tate and B.P.

In the concluding chapter, Victor Jeleniewski Seidler focuses on another facet of globally insistent corporateness. His text was sparked by exchanges and dialogues between himself and artist Ruth Maclennan. Central to their interaction is the exploration of the performative languages of corporateness, enhanced in this text by a meeting between sociology and contemporary arts practice. One of Ruth Maclennan's artworks discussed here is staged in a room at the LSE, an educational institution inextricably bound to the economies of corporateness. What unfolds is how interdisciplinarity resides here in a project of good listening. Interchange – between artist and artistic endeavour and sociology – draws attention to relationships between corporate language and its place in the interplay between – and construction of – subjectivities.

[1] David Cameron interviewed by Evan Davis on *The Today Programme*, BBC Radio 4, 17/04/13.

[2] R.Sennett, *Together: The Rituals, Pleasures and Politics of Cooperation*, Yale University Press, New Haven and London, 2012, p. ix.

[3] R.Sennett, p. 18.

Section One

— Pleasure and Fear in Interdisciplinary Arts Practice

Falling Together

— Carol Brown

The best way to collaborate is to choose the right person to collaborate with, and then trust them implicitly.[1]

Is there an inter-disciplinary body, capable of moving fluidly between discourses, disciplines, methods and processes? A body exceeding its own knowledge in the acquiring of the unfamiliar and in the inhabiting of the previously unknown? Perhaps the inter-disciplinary body is one without loyalty, without fidelity to any particular disciplinary technique or method; promiscuous, able to flirt and fall for a heterogeneous array of potential partners. Such transdisciplinarity might involve bodily knowing striated with the cross-hatchings of different discourses, drives and tactical displacements.

As a choreographer I generally collaborate with performers, designers, dramaturges and audiences to produce performance events through inter-subjective processes. Since 1999 these collaborations have broadened to include a variety of artists, researchers and practitioners whose work is not generally located in theatrical environments or arrived at through performance.[2] Alongside these collaborations I have, since 2002, engaged in inter-disciplinary performance research with architect and performance designer Dorita Hannah and sound artist Russell Scoones through M|A|P.[3] Our *dance-architectures* explore the intersection of the built environment's slow time with the varying temporalities of historical, aesthetic and embodied daily events through site-responsive performance (*Her Topia* 2005, *Aarero Stone* 2006, *Tongues of Stone* 2011 and *Mnemosyne* 2011). This shift from making work largely for theatre environments, where I was the main author, towards an expanded definition of choreography that emerges through collaborative practice, as dance-architecture, performance installation and site responsive event, has involved radically different forms of creation that test the corporeal and social limits of those involved.

Each of the inter-disciplinary collaborations I have engaged in, though wildly different in their constitutive components, involves a similar cycle of creation that likens the work to an emergent organism. This includes *co-conceiving* through connecting conversations, *developing* these ideas through

Section One — Pleasure and Fear in Interdisciplinary Arts Practice

Urban Devas 2010 Queen St,
Auckland, created by Carol Brown
and Phil Dadson for Living Room.
Photograph by Carol Brown.

SeaUnSea 2008 Choreography
Carol Brown, Design, Mette
Ramsgard Thomsen.
Photograph by Mattias Ek.

writing, sketching and designing, *embodying* the ideas, concepts or actions through *enfleshing* material in the studio or site, *creating compositional frames for* this material, *cultivating it* and *testing it out* in controlled conditions, (asking *does the idea have legs?*), and, *critical feeding back* into the performance system before making public as event. Each of these stages flexes and folds back onto each other as the cycle of each work gathers momentum. The heterogeneous languages solicited by inter-disciplinary processes together with the contradictions and unpredictable nature of inter-practice situations frequently makes for a messy and risky process snagged by misunderstandings, disciplinary differences and tensions around the diverse resource and material needs of the practices and practitioners involved. At the heart of this process however is the subjective agency of the dancer-performer to willingly engage and collaborate in the process or not.

Although my experience of inter-disciplinary practice takes manifold incarnations, I cannot talk about this work without also discussing the dancer-performers who embody it. For it is their bodies and corporeal signatures that instantiate the work. In choosing the labour of dancers, rather than actors, musicians or non-specialist bodies, in the making of work I am committed to an inter-practice process where *the situation of dancing* shapes the course and content of that action as much as any other element. This preference is not just the result of my own familiarity with contemporary dance, given a genealogy of practice as a dancer, but an acknowledgement of dancers' potentiality for multiple, protean incarnations and for a multiplicity of embodied expressions of body-site relations.[4] At the same time, I am curious about the agile mobility of dancers, (including myself) to work with and move through the logics of practices and processes alien to those dominantly incorporated through regimes of training in dance. Inter-disciplinary encounters in effect make strange what we already know. The contention is that the nomadic traversing of inter-practice environments is both risky and pleasurable and that, following the insights of my co-artists in other fields, contemporary dancing bodies, working as embodied subjects through processes of creation, can make *willing subjects* for inter-disciplinary environments.[5]

Section One — Pleasure and Fear in Interdisciplinary Arts Practice

Carol Brown performing
Mnemosyne 2011 created by Dorita
Hannah, Russell Scoones and Carol
Brown for Prague Quadrenniale
Photograph by Russell Scoones.

Mnemosyne 2011 created by Dorita
Hannah, Russell Scoones and Carol
Brown for Prague Quadrenniale
Photograph by Russell Scoones.

Freedom and Restraint in Becoming Willing

Being an inter-disciplinary artist can feel like being a trespasser in a foreign landscape, one who has to quickly learn the rules of a new and unfamiliar context to resist being exiled from what one knows. In this condition of unfamiliarity, I must learn how to apply myself as an embodied artist, to incorporate the local language to understand its codes and conventions, I must learn to reinvent myself and this changes the way I move. These transformations bring my body into a different status and set of alignments within the cultural field.

Given time to research in this unfamiliar context I borrow strategies, graft methods, translate between languages; my body becomes a conduit; a conductor mobilised by heterogeneous discourses and modes of practice. Moving with and from other disciplinary methods and applying these, radically un-houses what is known and familiar. This opens a critical creative space but also carries a risk of submission to the logics of an-other and a concomitant loss of agency.

The body of the dancer in inter-practice environments becomes the site of negotiation between the axes of materiality, imagination, resources and risk. As the sensory planes of different disciplines meet they affect each other creating new identities. The mutual imbrication of dance, music and architecture for instance, requires conceptual mapping and the possibility of the transfer of attributes from one field of practice onto another. This movement from a space of meeting to a blended space of conceptual integration requires skilled negotiation and openness but not necessarily ease. The un-ease of collaboration, experienced as opposition, resistance and primary disconnection, carries particular risks for dancers whose abilities to 'sign' their work is imbricated in the process of collaboration. The facility of dancers to create particular kinds of worlds emerges largely through the forms of complicity their collective working together generates. Gesa Ziemer[6] describes this complicity between dancers as enabling them to access the twilight zones, the fall and dive of collaborative process. As a tactic, complicity allows dancers to animate opportunities that arise, to combine unlikely elements and to create 'fissures and holes in the fabric of established systems'.[7]

The dancer who engages in an inter-disciplinary practice with multiple collaborators experiences a transgression of disciplinary borders and a pulverizing of the unity of their identity leading to the emergence of a new sense of agency. Through the dynamic interaction and counterpointing of different skills and expertise, something else, something unpredictable emerges. This might involve surprise, pain or delight and eventually comprehension of change.

Relearning Embodiment

Below are a number of examples of work tools I have used with dancers in the studio arising from collaborative conversations together with the names of the catalyzing conversant:

Discover balance at the edge of collapse (sculptor, Chris Booth)
Map the morphology of a virtual other to your anatomy (computer scientist, Chiron Mottram)
Use spline geometry to draw space around you (architect, Mette Ramsgard Thomsen)
Ask what is behind the image (performance designer, Dorita Hannah)
Create a pathway using the proof of irrational numbers (mathematician, Marcus du Sautoy)
Pixelate at a cellular level (architect, Mette Ramsgard Thomsen)
Create a movement score from sleep science data[8] (chronobiologist, Phillippa Gander)

Embodiment is relearned with each instance of choreography, shaping a reconstituted corporeal identity *that dances* between the logics of different disciplines. Each collaborative process takes place through a series of networks shaped by the coordinates of heterogeneous practices, over time these form a connective tissue within and between *us*. In this way a somatic language coheres, bonding previously disparate and separate elements, states and kinesthetic apparati. The affective charge of this process is underscored by the transgression of the known and is felt as moments of rupture, incongruity and heightened sensation.

It is this mix of language and material that constitutes the composting process of a new work but it is a partial element of a much larger gestalt shaped by the willingness of those involved to be receptive subjects capable of *dwelling* in the process of change.

Only if we are capable of dwelling, only then can we build.[9]

Performers engaged in inter-disciplinary projects become the hosts, receivers, developers and interpreters of diverse discourses and practices but they must also *inhabit* what they *build*. Tim Etchells describes the performing artist as 'a kind of receiver', like a 'sensing device' who allows him or herself to be spoken through. It is in this state of responsiveness that discoveries are made:

> I know that we go to the rehearsal studio in the first instance not knowing what we intend and not knowing where we are going with the work. The rehearsal process is a kind of stumbling, a discovering and to a certain extent a channeling of what's in the air between us and around us. In a certain way I don't feel 100 percent in control of that process and that's fine because I really don't quite trust or believe 'intentions'. I think a lack of control or certainty can be important in fact, because it allows you a sensitivity to possibilities or ideas that you don't really understand or which you don't necessarily recognize at first.[10]

Etchells describes uncertainty and sensitivity to what emerges in the studio as essential to Forced Entertainment's inter-disciplinary theatre as well as a kind of free-fall in the act of stumbling. I stumble around the studio waiting to be tripped up by something unexpected. I also seem to stumble into collaborations that take me places unanticipated. Liz created a blind date for Esther and I; Stewart introduced me to his former girlfriend Mette one night at his flat in West London; Dorita and I met through a British Council supported visit to Prague. Collaborations are initiated through unpredictable encounters but also, increasingly through curatorial strategies to 'match-make' artists with box office appeal for diverse audiences.[11]

Collaborative Praxes

Dance philosopher, Anna Pakes, writes on the tacit knowledge employed in studio practice environments through the process of building a work. Inter-disciplinary collaborators in the studio often include artists and researchers from disciplines unfamiliar with performance making processes. 'Creative sensitivity' to others, the emerging situation and the experiences this generates is crucial to the process (although easily overlooked when under pressure to get work off the ground). For Pakes this 'creative sensitivity' lies in collaborators' ability to recognise what a process is suggesting to be the 'right' course of action. Decisions emerge from circumstances and are sensitive to the contingencies and evolution of working relationships. She describes this form of practical wisdom as *phronesis*, a type of knowledge developed by Aristotle and associated with *praxis*. *Phronesis* acknowledges 'the variable and mutable world of human beings' as it emerges through inter-subjective action and encounters. What is required in this domain is *'a creative sensitivity to circumstances as they present themselves'* (italics mine). *Phronesis* in this way is described as:

> ...requiring subjective involvement rather than objective detachment; and it has an irreducibly personal dimension in its dependence upon, and the fact that it folds back into, subjective and intersubjective experience.[12]

At the heart of inter-disciplinary collaboration is an inter-subjective matrix informed by the desires, intentions, affects, and moods of those involved. If, following Heidegger, it is through 'bare mood' that what matters to us can be encountered[13] and as Pakes proposes, *a state of attunement* is essential to successful collaboration.[14] It is this state through which discoveries can be made. Although this state may in practice move between serenity and anxiety, it allows space for a pleasurable immersion in the process of becoming together. In contrast, a process of mis-attunement might be one in which the artists and researchers in the project fail to connect, where those involved may feel misunderstood. Recent research into kinesthetic empathy reinforces the view that to be truly inter-subjective we need to be empathetically engaged.[15]

Finding Reverie

Perhaps, dancers, with their propensity for becoming *willing subjects* can enable inter-practice situations precisely because they quickly drop into a kinesthetic or somatic state which goes beyond rational thought, to readily sense the inter-subjective cues between each other. At some point in the process, as a choreographer working with dancers I have to stop talking and speculating and pay attention to the emergent sensations and developing somatic language in the room. This shift in state is a powerful letting go, a releasing of energy and a listening; it can induce a state of reverie:

Tongues of Stone 2011 created by
Dorita Hannah, Carol Brown and
Russell Scoones for STRUT.
Photo by Christophe Canato

Perth Institute of Contemporary
Arts, Professional Development
Workshop for STRUT.
Photo by Mette Ramgsard Thomsen.

[Reverie] captures something of a dream state and yet it is not sleep. It is a state of absorption or play, and it is also serious; it conjures a state of not quite being in the world, [....] it is in reverie that life is often at its most vivid and alive. It is if you like, an in-between state. A state that resists narrative, or at least disturbs and unsettles it. And that dissolves the distinction between thinking and feeling, between watching and experiencing.[16]

In the studio, the complicity of the dancers creates micro situations of intimacy where digressions, off-topic slippages, jokes and confidences arise in the spaces and stillnesses between tasks. These gaps in the logic of constructing a work can be seen as openings towards transitional spaces.

For the psychoanalyst, Donald Winnicott, transitional spaces are intermediate zones inextricably linked to play and creativity. Transitional phenomena originate in the child's capacity to play creatively in the private world that is allowed to her, or to him, by the holding presence of the primary caregiver.[17] The transitional state is a relational site, neither completely subjective nor objective; it is a potential space for the imagination. This capacity, to be held in a transitional site that allows relaxation into being with the other, is a joint condition through which we are alive to the world and the world is alive to us. Yet these states cannot be accessed readily within a tight and pressured schedule of rehearsal, which allows little room for stumbling around, and the free-fall of playing together.

From *Now* to *Next*

From my perspective, the experience of co-creation is fostered best when there is space for play. The *situation of dancing* as a non-verbal state that shifts us off-balance, opens the possibility of stumbling, faltering, falling and playing, offers a particular kind of potential for inter-disciplinary collaboration through the reverie of attunement to the rhythms of an-other.

As a choreographer, I search for moments of *now* when there is a feeling in the room that palpably cuts through the stress of co-creation, when we can relax into the arrival of something unforeseen. A *now* moment can get emotionally charged, suddenly everything hangs in the balance. Nothing else is happening except the present moment; these are extreme *now* moments that perturb and unsettle the pattern of moving and relating. In these moments I sense a need for resolution of some kind. The most unsuccessful will be an impasse, a missed opportunity when perhaps surprise, embarrassment or shame overwhelms the charged moment and we move onto some more familiar ground. These moments of meeting through interdisciplinary practice change us and the way we make and perceive what we do. In a sense they undo us.[18]

Surrender without Sacrifice

Moving beyond the dialectics of inside and outside, it is important to consider how a dancer engaged in inter-disciplinary practice surrenders to a process without sacrificing the opportunity for subjectivisation through it. If I surrender to the task of being in the now, what does this moment solicit from me?

In the worldmaking of collaborative practice the labour of dancers has strong potential to galvanise a process given their kinesthetic intelligence carries the capacity for quick actions and reactions. Through inter-disciplinary practice the predominantly nonverbal practice of dancing meets and negotiates the symbolic systems of other disciplinary activities. This involves frequent crossings between discursive, kinesthetic, material and libidinal economies. Creating an environment which is conducive to risk-taking and discovery involves trust, an attunement to each other and the making of a space for genuine meeting and play. The micro-movements of this space as a relational site are primordial to the encounter and can be said, to determine what is made possible within it. Opening up a space within which things can appear is a dynamic process of gathering, co-extensive action and a technique of *letting-dwell*.[19]

Inter-disciplinary practice incorporating dancing bodies creates an expanded field for choreography beyond the representation of any one particular form. The pliability of the dancer in for instance embodying architectural spaces, working prosthetically through interactive technologies, sounding their skin-sense in sonic worlds can be disarming as she/he refuses to be singularly identified as an expert practitioner of one kind. Immersed in ongoing somatic enquiries, contemporary dancers often appear *willing* to take risks and collaborate on the terms defined by other fields.

Distracting oneself from the corporeal *now* to engage in performative dialogues with other disciplines can generate a renewed appreciation for the possibilities of dance as a way of making thinking fluid in the space of the *next*.

Desiring somatic subjects seek out moments of surrender within alternative habitations, as dance is not containable within the object-centred discourses of dance as theatre practice. Unbound from the theatre as horizon, dancers who work within inter-disciplinary environments in the expanded field of performance experience discomfit. This productive violence shatters established modes of practice and changes the subjectivity of the dancer as well as that which is danced.[20]

Dances that involve touch depend on a shift of weight to a shared mobile centre or centres. You are no longer standing on your own two feet; the ground is shared and support is mutually reinforced. From this point of contact I can release into a supported fall or I can resist, pushing and pressing away to extend the arc of movement in another dimension or spatial plane. This is the pleasure when working in an inter-disciplinary way; the pull and push, attraction and repulsion of a duet dance redefining itself across a threshold of contact, at times pliable and at others frictive.

Friendship

If sensitivity through attunement and reverie are conducive to successful inter-disciplinary processes, other aspects can evolve through the specific kinds of conviviality and exchange opened by collaboration. A form of conviviality not unlike a friendship. Friendship is generally understood as a sustained relation where trust, reciprocity and empathy allow for meeting and separation, mingling and distance between equals. Performance scholar Joe Kelleher in discussing the idea of an 'affective archive' indicates the capacity in friendships for strangeness, disillusionment and being alone.[21] Describing Forced Entertainment's process of over 25 years, Kelleher suggests they created a way of working together that we could call friendship. A friendship that exceeds the affective bonds of closeness and might encompass indifference as well as autonomy.

It is perhaps unsurprising that sustained collaborations generate strong friendships. Friendships that emerge from inter-disciplinary collaborations are ones that preserve an autonomy but allow for the kind of indifference that lets us get on with the work of making. Such friendships can become as Deleuze put it, 'a condition of possibility of thought itself'.[22]

Conclusion

This essay argues that spatial understanding and kinesthetic knowledge that comes with dance training shapes dancers into willing risk-taking subjects for inter-disciplinary conversations but this fluency also brings the risk of being subjugated to the logics of another. Negotiating difference between disciplines becomes a process of becoming together. This process, reliant upon negotiation of differences, does not privilege linguistic signification — instead it acknowledges both the symbolic and pre-symbolic potential of corporeal knowing through processes of attunement and *letting-dwell* realised in the transitional spaces of inter-practice environments. The analogy of partnering skills in dance, to yield, resist, fall, surrender, merge and separate, forms a backbone to the essay as it leans towards a better understanding of the fears and pleasures that accompany inter-disciplinary work.

Finally, it is strong enduring friendships that shape forms of sociality beyond institutionalised models of attachment

[1] Kevin Volans cited in J. Burrows, *A Choreographer's Handbook*, Routledge, London and New York, 2010, p. 5.

[2] They include the visual artist Esther Rolinson (*Shelf Life* 1999 and *Machine for Living* 2001), architect Stewart Dodd (*Nerve* 2002) and Mette Ramsgard-Thomsen (*The Changing Room* 2004 and *SeaUnSea* 2006), mathematician Marcus du Sautoy (*The 19th Step* 2008), and chronobiologist Philippa Gander (*Revolve* 2011).

[3] Movement | Architecture | Performance is a locus for our research. We have co-conceived *dance-architectures* as spaces of encounter which go beyond the making of a dance or a building to explore performance as a critical spatial practice arising from specific narratives of embodiment within public space and the built environment.

[4] S. Foster, 'Dancing Bodies' in *Incorporations* (Zone 6), J. Crary and S. Kwinter (eds) MA: Zone/MIT Press, Cambridge, 1992, pp. 480-495.

[5] '*They are so willing*' was a frequently made statement by Dorita Hannah, a co-artist in M|A|P during the making of *Tongues of Stone* for STRUT Dance (Perth, 2011).

[6] G. Ziemer, 'Situational Worlds, Complicity as a Model of Collaboration' in *Emerging Bodies: The Performance of Worldmaking in Dance and Choreography*, G. Klein & S. Noeth (eds), Transcript Verlag, Bielefeld, 2011, pp. 235-245.

[7] Ziemer, p. 240.

[8] Examples of choreographic tasks and methods used in making *The Changing Room* (2005), *SeaUnSea* (2008), *The 19th Step* (2008), and *Aarero Stone* (2006).

[9] M. Heidegger, 'Building, Dwelling, Thinking' in *Basic Writings: Martin Heidegger*, D. Farrell Krell (ed) Routledge, London and New York, 1993, pp. 343-363.

[10] T. Etchells in H. Ploebst, *Tim Etchells on His Way Home – About "Spectacular" and other realms of Ghostliness*, 2008 viewed 6 July 2011. http://www.corpusweb.net/dd2-the-way-home.html

[11] Sadlers Wells Artistic Director Alistair Spalding has been responsible in the UK over recent years for putting together unexpected combinations of artists in high-profile collaborations including Sidi Larbi Cherkaoui, Antony Gormley and Nitin Sawhney's *Zero Degrees*. Other collaborations arise from more prosaic encounters, Anna Huber describes, 'Fritz Hauser came to one of my premieres because somebody said he makes music the way I dance. That's how our collaboration began.' (Weber/Ziemer 2007: n.p.).

[12] A. Pakes, 'Knowing through dance-making: Choreography, practical knowledge and practice-as-research', in *Contemporary Choreography: A Critical Reader*, J. Butterworth & L. Wildschut (eds), Routledge, London and New York, 2009, pp. 10-22.

[13] Heidegger in *Being and Time* explains the concept of '*Stimmung*', mood, and '*Gestimmtsein*' being-attuned, as opening spaces for discovery, '*Existentially, a state-of-mind implies a disclosive submission to the world, out of which we can encounter something that matters to us.*' (Camelot Press, London and Southampton, 1962, p. 177).

[14] A. Pakes, p. 18.

[15] Neuroscience provides a psychobiological basis for intersubjectivity. Research into watching movement has indicated that through a state of kinesthetic empathy mirror neurons fire in the brain as if you are doing what the other person you are observing does. This means you unconsciously participate in the other's experience. See for example, G. Rizzolatti and L. Craighero, 'The Mirror-Neuron System' *Annual Review of Neuroscience* vol. 27, July 2004, pp. 169-192.

[16] D. Modjeska, *Stravinsky's Lunch*, Picador, Sydney, 2001, p. 309.

[17] D. Winnicott, 'Transitional Objects and Transitional Phenomena'. *International Journal of Psychoanalysis*, 1953, 34, pp. 89-97.

[18] Heidegger suggests that the artist is largely inconsequential, a passageway, and destroys itself in order for the work to emerge. See M. Heidegger, *The Question Concerning Technology and Other Essays*, trans. W. Lovitt, Garland, New York, 1977.

[19] For Heidegger the essence of building is *letting-dwell* which he describes as a *techné*. For the Greeks *techné* is neither art nor handicraft but making something appear within what is present (Heidegger in Farrell Krell, p. 361).

[20] Estelle Barrett, citing Kristeva describes the practice of art as 'a kind of productive violence that shatters established discourse and in doing so changes the status of the subject and its relation to the body, to others and to objects' E. Barrett, *Kristeva Reframed*, I.B.Tauris, London and New York, 2011, p. 13.

[21] J. Kelleher, 'On Friendship' Unpublished Paper presented as part of Performance Symposium, Auckland University of Technology, 28 July 2011.

[22] G. Deleuze & F. Guattari, *What is Philosophy?* Colombia University, New York, 1994, p. 3.

Department 21

— Bianca Elzenbaumer and Fabio Franz (Brave New Alps) in conversation with Laura Mansfield

Bianca Elzenbaumer and Fabio Franz were invited to speak at a symposium exploring ideas of 'Art School alternatives' held at Liverpool John Moores University in November 2010 as part of the activities surrounding the publication *Corridor 8.*[1] The notion of an 'alternative' art school — particularly models involving peer-to-peer learning that challenged institutional frameworks — had become a talking point. At a moment when the financial cost of higher education was increasing significantly, students and artists were questioning the institutional structures on offer. While studying for an MA in Communication Art and Design at the Royal College of Art, Elzenbaumer and Franz's ambitious project, 'Department 21' was initiated with a number of other students. They sought to create a new interdisciplinary department within the institutions' 20 segregated disciplines. It became a space for sharing, discussion and collaboration between students from a range of different subjects.

In their publication about the development of the Department 21 project Bianca Elzenbaumer, Stephen Knott and Polly Hunter discuss the notion of interdisciplinarity:

> Interdisciplinarity is essentially an exercise in de-territorialisation, giving up space and sacrificing something. … How else do you create de-territorialised spaces and objects? One strategy is to relinquish authorship. Another is to adopt a different set of tools. As tools provide the security that allows individuals to respond to any given problem, practitioners hide behind them. In contrast collaborative labour provides a respect and an understanding of another way of approaching a subject.[2]

The notion of de-territorialisation implies a military maneouvre suggesting the struggle, battle and conflict that can

Section One — Pleasure and Fear in Interdisciplinary Arts Practice

Chalk boards.
(Photo: Department 21)

Department 21 work space in the
former Painting studio — 2010
(Photo: Department 21)

occur in an effort to maintain your own identity and discipline while learning from, and incorporating, the structures, language and methods of another. It is a space of both conflict and learning that can facilitate a collaborative labour.

On graduating Elzenbaumer and Franz secured the continuation of Department 21 for the 2010/11 academic year, with the project being led and shaped by a new wave of students, continuing as a recognised part of the formal Art School structure.

LM — Can you start by explaining a little about Brave New Alps and your design practice before you went to the RCA — have you always had an interest in interdisciplinarity? How did your work/projects reflect that notion of interdisciplinarity?

BNA — We started working together as Brave New Alps in 2005, when we were preparing the final thesis for our BA in Design at the Free University of Bozen-Bolzano in Italy. While studying a mixture of communication and product design, in a faculty whose structure was very focused on issue-specific rather than discipline-specific projects, we realised that we both had a very keen interest in using our design tools as a means of contributing to a variety of critical discourses.

For every project on the course, we were asked to research a new topic, for example, networks or branding, and were required to respond to the topic with the medium that seemed most appropriate. Collaborating was a good way of complementing each other's design skills.

Alongside the issue-specific focus of our BA, which made us quite naturally cross over between two design disciplines, the particularity of the University's tiny design faculty made us curious about the other subjects being taught. Sitting amongst economy, agriculture, informatics and educational science the position of the design faculty made us very interested in what these other students were learning and what we could learn from them, especially as we needed to research a new social or political issue every term. We simply saw a huge potential in tapping into the knowledge and viewpoints of people with different backgrounds as it gave us fresh insights into something we were working on. For example, for our final thesis we worked with a regional green politician, a tourism anthropologist, a tiered environmental activist and the director of a museum of tourism among others. Here, the specific knowledge of these people was woven into our

Section One — Pleasure and Fear in Interdisciplinary Arts Practice

Department 21 publication
(Photo: Department 21)

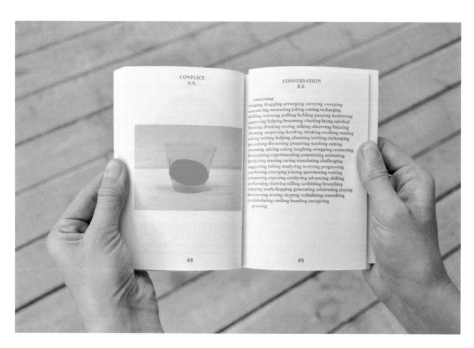

Department 21 publication
(Photo: Department 21)

projects; *intacta Ltd.*, a fake, but very aggressive tourism company that we launched on the regional media; and *Brave New Winter*, a travelling exhibition reflecting on how the climatic conditions of winter are manipulated through artificial snow-making, which in turn alters perceptions of nature.

LM — Did your enthusiasm to learn from different disciplines and engage with other fields of knowledge in the formation of your projects continue once at the RCA?
Did the different environment of the College facilitate and support or disrupt and disable your interdisciplinary working method?

BNA — We decided to apply to the RCA because of the variety of design disciplines represented within the College. Furthermore, we were fascinated by the praise of interdisciplinary learning promoted on the college's website. Coming from a tiny faculty, we were eager to meet and work with architects, curators and design historians and have the opportunity to find out about contemporary ceramics, textiles, jewellery and finally getting to work, if not with, then at least beside, fine artists. We pretty soon came back down to earth, realising that the interdisciplinarity described in the prospectus was an idea in which the College liked to indulge, rather than an actuality.

We had the impression that we would be joining the RCA as a whole, but once inside we soon realised that we had actually only joined the department of Communication Art & Design, as the College is structured into Schools, which are further subdivided into departments. Each department – there are 20 of them – has its own budget and own agenda, which is jealously looked after. This sensation of subdivision is further underlined by the fact that without the right student card you cannot physically access the studios of certain departments, although we are all part of the same, rather small college.

It felt as if the opening up of an interdisciplinary department would only interfere with the delivery of the educational plan: the specialisation of students within one discipline and the presentation of a strong Final Show. Consequently, if you are one of those students who want to move on in their practice not by specialisation, but by broadening your understanding of cultural production in a wider sense, you are pretty much up against a system that believes that the further you advance within your studies the narrower your focus needs to be. It's a system that pushes interdisciplinarity only when it makes 'logical sense', assuming that an industrial design engineer has a lot to share with a vehicle designer, but dismissing any chance that a vehicle designer might prefer to exchange ideas with a printmaker.

LM — in your publication about the Department 21 project you state that:

The interdisciplinary method prompts unease – there is the danger of being so in-between that no one accepts you into their field, your skills find no natural home. But it is a risk worth taking, and is a way of stretching the terrain between disciplinary boundaries.[3]

LM — You're talking here about your own unease at not knowing whether you would meet resistance and also the potential unease of those who might reject your offer of interaction, (elsewhere you mention 'departmental inhibitions'). How were these fears overcome on both sides?

BNA — We spent our first year at the RCA trying to get our heads around the organisation of the college, realising that if we did not want to spend two years learning only from the people in our own department we needed to organise some sort of exchange on our own.

Certainly at the beginning we felt an unease in not knowing if other students would join for such an open and not output-focused interdisciplinary exchange. But this unease on our side was on the one hand simply overcome by our curiosity and desire to learn from others in unexpected ways, on the other hand it was overcome because we met students from other departments who also embraced our approach. Regarding the unease on the side of the institution we are not sure how things developed. To us it almost seems that where unease existed it remained due to very little engagement with what we did, whereas there were those within the institution who felt just as curious as us to see what such an interdisciplinary approach could lead to within a place like the Royal College of Art.

We started by setting up a one day skills exchange at the end of the first year in order to test if a format of peer-to-peer learning could work, and if the current students would be keen

Department 21 – Bianca Elzenbaumer and Fabio Franz (Brave New Alps) in conversation with Laura Mansfield

Department 21 at RCA Show 2011 – Designing the Design Process – 2011
(Photo: Department 21)

Department 21 installation at RCA
Show 2010
(Photo: Department 21)

to participate. Energised by this experience, over the summer we made contact with students from other departments in order to organise a longer workshop in one of the college's corridors – called the Hockney Gallery. At the beginning of October 2009, together with Ana Viegas and approximately 30 more students most of whom we barely knew, we organised *stop.swap.*

For the duration of five days, *stop.swap.* transformed the Hockney Gallery corridor into a laboratory for exchange: with a communal breakfast in the morning, several student-led workshops throughout the day and a screening in the evening. The students running workshop sessions were from Communication Art & Design, Textiles, Design Products, Goldsmithing, Photography, Design Interaction, History of Design and Animation. The activities proposed ranged from in-depth presentations of working methods over collective live animations, to practical exercises in colour theory. *stop.swap.* enabled us to finally find out more about the processes adopted by different disciplines and discover what concerns underlaid the differing students' personal work and wider field of practice. This first exchange further formed the basis upon which we looked to build a more permanent platform for shared exchanges between students from different departments and disciplines.

LM — Was this knowledge something that you directly used in the development of your own practice, or rather is the facilitation of an opening up and sharing of knowledge a central drive within your own practice?

BNA — By getting to know other students' approaches, we were able to diversify our own ways of operating, giving us the confidence to step out of our ingrained ways of doing things. The opening up and sharing of ideas, approaches and practices is also a mode of interaction that fosters the development of an active creative environment that reflects our approach to living and working together in general. We like to think that great projects don't grow out of the isolation and protection of ideas, but out of sharing them with others. Once an idea is 'put out there' it can be discussed from a variety of viewpoints, there can be multiple ways of contributing to it or developing it further. For us, this shared process results in strong projects that are supported not only by a single person but by a community bound together by trust. The process of sharing ideas and building up a common project takes time in order to not simply be a utilitarian finalisation of a common goal. Time allows for building up relationships on which further common plans can be constructed and which provide support in 'rough' times.

LM — The community of support you are describing, that forms through working with others who have a specific knowledge and specialism is also a community that is sharing a learning process. The introduction to different viewpoints and ideas expands an individual's perception and knowledge base. Do you think the shared way of working you describe can be adopted as a model for other disciplines outside of your own practice?

BNA — We believe that this shared way of working can and should be adopted for and among other disciplines. Education within any discipline provides and teaches different ways of approaching problems and concerns, specific vocabularies for talking about the world, and very distinct fields of knowledge. The possibility of bringing together people from a great variety of backgrounds can open up new ways of seeing and thinking about the world.

This process of the sharing of knowledge between individuals from different backgrounds takes more time than that required for the sharing of knowledge between people who are building up from a very similar grounding. Exchange between different fields is less streamlined and more complex – and we would say that it actually better reflects the professional context encountered outside education, which is similarly complex, requiring a number of stakeholders and factors to be considered.

We have also found that researchers in both science and the humanities often have difficulty opening up their findings to both the wider public and to professionals working in neighbouring fields. Involving a designer right from the beginning, who accompanies the whole project and is focused on how the research can be communicated to the outside world, could be part of a very interesting and fruitful process.

In terms of involving the surrounding community in the design process, we are very interested in models that experiment with new structures of consensus building and direct democracy. Here we find it exciting to work with sociologists and mediators, who are researching alternative social models. In fact, Bianca has completed an MA in Mediation and Peacekeeping where she worked and studied with — among others — sociologists, anthropologists and lawyers. We collaborated on projects like *Fortezza Open Archive*[4], where we have been actively participating with the community to develop planning visions for the future of a tiny village in the Alps, whose economic basis, connected to railway transport, has collapsed.

Through these experiences we found ourselves influenced by the often very unconventional situations these practitioners created to get communication going between people. The results of such a participatory planning process often suit the project's purpose better than a solution planned in a rather sterile studio. However, they are not necessarily suitable for a process oriented towards profit and tight deadlines.

LM — In your Department 21 publication you mention cultivating 'conviviality' as a means to create 'the context for hybrid identities to develop, rooted in mutual support'[5]. Is this an indicator of where the pleasure lies for you in the processes of interdisciplinarity?

To us the cultivation of conviviality was crucial but it was also one of the things we got most criticised for. This criticism was mostly directed at the "unproductivity" of conviviality. Just being together, getting to know each other and exchanging thoughts in a not-outcome-focussed way might have been seen as being besides the point of a career-oriented education. But for us, it was these moments of being together without the pressure to perform in the usual way that made this educational experience even more valuable. We are not sure if conviviality is automatically part of a process of interdisciplinarity, but an interdisciplinary setting can help to bring people together in a more exploratory way and this is something we enjoy and value precisely because it is not productive in a straightforward way.

This interview took place in November 2010.

Bianca Elzenbaumer is currently studying for a PhD at Goldsmiths College London, while still working collaboratively with Fabio Franz. Department 21 is continuing at the Royal College of Art with students from the new academic year coordinated by Bethany Wells and Sophie Demay.

In 2009/2010 Department 21 was an initiative by Bianca Elzenbaumer & Fabio Franz (Brave New Alps, Communication Art & Design), Polly Hunter (History of Design), Callum Cooper (Animation), Carmen Billows (Curating Contemporary Art), Anais Tondeur (Textiles), Sara Muzio (Animation), Melissa Gamwell (Ceramics), Ottilie Ventiroso & Oliver Wainwright (Architecture).

www.brave-new-alps.com

www.department21.net

[1] R. McKinley and M. Butterworth (eds), *Corridor 8, The Borderlands Edition*, Manchester, October 2010.

[2] B. Elzenbaumer, F. Franz and P. Hunter (eds), *Department 21*, London, June 2010, p. 68.

[3] Elzenbaumer, Franz and Hunter, p. 69.

[4] *Fortezza Open Archive* was a project by Brave New Alps in collaboration with the Municipality of Franzensfeste-Fortezza for Manifesta 7, the European biennial of contemporary art, which took place in Trentino-Südtirol from 19 July to 2 November 2008.

[5] Elzenbaumer, Franz and Hunter, p. 1.

Shoreline and Sea

— Jane Calow

Embarking upon an heuristic voyage: *a lull on the journey in which to consider an artwork in construction… **Mantle***

This text is a reflection on my artistic practice that embraces possibilities offered by interdisciplinary research, discourse, collaboration, negotiation and physical making. The enquiry draws upon Geology, Geography, Psychoanalysis, Language and Epistemology. This imaged text is a muse upon *Mantle*; it is in itself a poetics, a sketch in progress, reflection upon which encompasses the multifarious conditions of beginnings and possible resolutions of a way through to the production of a coherent artwork. What triggers the start of making? What possible continuities can lead towards production?

I am linked by birth to the North East of England. The harshness of life for working class people at a certain socio-historic moment within the economic conditions of a time (the interwar years) has been vividly conveyed to me. The legacy that has been handed on is freighted. Something that is part of my mythology is a set of stories that recount few choices. These are neo-historic narratives that touch upon stories that are close, that become absorbed within a dynamic that touches and permeates my being. All of us are part of and recount narratives of being: about ourselves to ourselves and to others. Mine is en-knotted with shore and sea.

The search for origins is tempting but illusory. In intellectual matters absolute beginnings are exceedingly rare. We find, instead continuities and breaks. New interventions reflect events outside a discipline but have effects within it. They most often work to reorganise a set of problems or field of inquiry. They reconstitute existing knowledge under the sign of new questions. They dispose existing elements into new configurations, establish new points of departure.[1]

A point of departure...

Mantle is artwork driven by a preoccupation with lost bodies. It stems from close proximity with the sea and sea-faring communities. *Mantle* was triggered by an engagement with a specific geological phenomenon and place. It is underpinned by an intimate story about class, migration, mourning and grief and the difficulties of finding means of articulation through a range of forms of representation. It is work informed by psychoanalysis intimately enmeshed with social, cultural, historic and geographical specificity; it touches both physical and psychic spatialisations[2]. I am drawn towards the possibility of emergent representational forms; looking towards entwining what is intimate with what might emerge as public; a far and near. This lull in the voyage offers the possibility to consider what might be reached through thought, action, transposition and making – engagement with lived experiences.

This is a narrative of a bumpy, hopeful methodological journey towards the anchoring of an articulated artwork – an attempt to place a personal account of a practice firmly within interdisciplinarity. Within the context of *Mantle*, interdisciplinarity is imperative; *Mantle* is a journeying with what is predicated upon complex physicalities yet notes what can appear within peripheral vision: a sideways glance – what may flicker at the edges... Within the very nature of engagement with interdisciplinarity it is to simultaneously face the trepidation and potential pleasures of meandering into uncharted territories. Working in the direction of the articulation of *Mantle* has lead to speaking with and recording communities, working towards constructing musical composition and the prospect of working with musicians and technologies that encompass image making and filmmaking. At many points along this journey it is necessary to acknowledge the place of the expertise of others, to demur to deep knowledge within other disciplines and to hand over work, with grace, to individuals who have expertise. It is to recognise one's own limitations and the limitations of the discipline within which one finds oneself.

..... all this is happening in conjunction with finding orientation – not least, thinking the vastness of the Atlantic...

  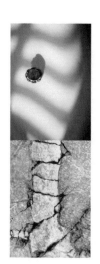

Untitled, Victorian mourning brooch containing pearls
and hair with the Mantle of the Earth at Coverack.
(Image: Jane Calow)

Section One — Pleasure and Fear in Interdisciplinary Arts Practice

Newlyn Harbour. (Image: Jane Calow)

Sea change – a matter of moving waters... migrations and condensations

These notes on migrations and condensations were prompted by a conversation with a geographer, where the physics of condensation and its place within the discipline of physical geography were explained to me in terms that I can begin to understand and relate to – terms from somewhere else – an Other disciplinarity. This is an exciting encounter that activates the possibility of connections between disciplines that might contribute to processes of producing my artwork and offer a space for contemplation upon my own migratings. This is apropos consideration of intersections with other theorisations of states of being, thinking and encounters with the material world; my own encounter with the concept of condensation comes from psychoanalysis.

What occurs to me in the process of thinking interdisciplinarity is not only the associated practicalities – the nuts and bolts of negotiating across disciplinary borders – but also the internality of certain disciplines that find recourse to draw upon other disciplines. Perhaps through resonance, metaphor, rapport and analogy navigational pathways may be opened up between disciplines that accordingly lead towards possible surfacing and subsequent provision for the articulation of unanticipated vivid forms of representation.

For me, physical and psychic space (both the physical world and the conscious body coupled with the unconscious) are inter-related; they are connected by spatialisation, which in my art making draws together specific sites of inquiry and physicality that in turn inform and prompt new inquiries and offer possible routes to find associative chains through to art work.

Considering the world and abstraction: physics, physical geographies and psychoanalysis

Within a scientific explanation, water is the only substance that exists in three states – solid, liquid and vapour – all in close proximity at the same time. With an energy input, ice (solid water) increases in temperature up to melting point, where further energy input will be used to turn the ice into water (liquid). This water will rise in temperature by 100 degrees Centigrade if the energy input continues until evaporation point (or 'boiling point') is reached and the continuing energy input is used to turn the liquid water into water vapour. Water temperature doesn't change at evaporation point despite the continuing energy input, which doesn't show on the temperature scale but is stored in the resultant water vapour as 'latent heat of evaporation'. This latent heat energy remains 'hidden' in the water vapour until the latter loses energy and cools (soon after energy input ceases for any reason) and condenses, at which point it is released from its hidden store into the air surrounding the tiny floating droplets of water (cloud). This physical process is the geographers' explanation for the avalanche-producing warm descending winds such as the Fohn in the French Alps and the Chinook in the North American Rockies.

Latency and hidden energy: condensation

The constructs of the release of energy and latency – indications of transformative processes that carry intimations of internality and externality – are apparent within another deployment of the term condensation. Latency and condensation are constructs reconfigured and applied by Sigmund Freud to modes of the functioning of unconscious processes. Condensation is one of the foundations of the fundamental workings of unconscious process; along with the construct of displacement, Freud writes of it in conjunction to dream work and cathexis: '...the fact that a certain amount of physical energy is attached to an idea or to a group of ideas, to a part of the body, to an object, etc.'[3]

What the combination of condensation and cathexis convey is complex processes interconnecting visceral, embodied lived experience and mental work. Finding analogies across disciplines links experience to the interpretation of the physical world.

How we communicate across disciplines is subtly nuanced, providing interstices where latency exists; gaps – rich in opportunities for meetings and migrations.

Journeying hopefully...

Returning to standing on the shoreline. Let us begin again; I will attempt a plotting – a mapping. *Mantle* was sparked by an encounter in Cornwall, at Coverack, a place where the mantle of the earth breaks through its crust.

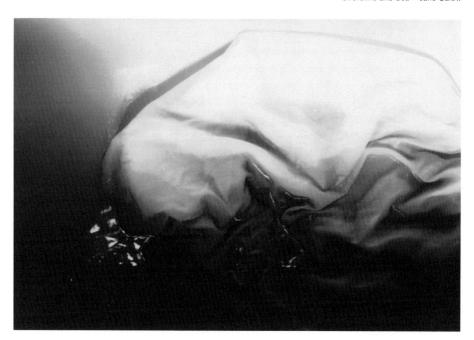

Shroud. (Image: Jane Calow)

The mantle surfaces; at first this place may appear unremarkable.
A small shingle beach with detritus washed ashore. Meanwhile,
crossing the Atlantic the mantle surfaces at Trout Bay, Newfoundland.
Coverack and Trout Bay have rapport – they both hold closeness to
places of fishing and community and the eruption, the breaching of a
physical surface, where the mantle of the earth breaks through the crust
of the earth; a meeting across the Atlantic.

Surfacing

Geologically, Coverack is of world import. I wouldn't know this
but for the pleasure and privilege of having my good friend the
geographer to hand and meeting people who could interpret and
communicate the subtle geographies and geology of this place.
Immediately after this experience I had to run to language and
epistemology, in order to research definition, classification and
associations. My aim was to think how *Mantle* might, through
migration across and between disciplines and other encounters
and conversations, emerge as an artwork. Attention and
sensitivity to the deep physical and social traces characterised
and formed through place and site are vital; I find myself
attuned to the approach of physical and cultural geographers and
psychogeographers; something that resonates with other ways of
thinking and making. In *A Skin for Thought* the psychoanalyst
Didier Anzieu articulates the fragility of the ego skin, where holes
– breaching – may occur.[4] The analogies between the meeting of
psychic and physical conditions and materiality prompted by this
remarkable place; the breaching of the crust of the earth by the
mantle at Coverack – a physical surfacing – and the breaching of
psyche thought through Anzieu, find some kind of meeting in the
geological guide to this part of Cornwall. It is a simple association.
The title of the guide is the *Skin of the Lizard*, conveying the
vulnerability of earth close to the sea, the vulnerability of the
visceral and psychic position of working people.

Making

Certain core values have threaded through my artistic practice
and have remained as preoccupations within the many
reconsiderations, revisions, reconstructions and adaptations that
are part and parcel of any reflective art practice. A commitment
to engagement with different constituencies and communities

that stand aside from the hegemonic processes of arts and their industries forms one of the many strong threads that inform and bind my work together. In a previous historical moment I was a painter with an investment in social realism. Coverack is in close proximity to the working harbour of Newlyn. I have long been interested in the Newlyn School of painters. What is striking about the Newlyn School is their concentration upon shoreline activity, whether it be the hard won delivery of fish to the quay, or interiors of homes, or the sentimental yet dramatic depiction of women waiting on the shore for their men to return, or 'the old sailor' safe, finally at comfort within the community. All this occurs on dry land, albeit taking in shoreline – an edgeland, an in-between far away from the activities of being at sea.

Uncharted waters....

For those who die at sea there may be no body – nobody – no means through which to grieve or structure mourning for those left bereft at shore. This is the experience, along with long periods of absence with which fishing communities are familiar. In Newlyn, within the Fisherman's Mission (a place I was privileged enough to enter and talk to and record a number of Skippers, where they candidly spoke about the fabric of their lives) there is a room of commemoration and contemplation for families. This commemorative quiet place offers room to consider loss; a place set aside for grieving, mourning and perhaps the possibility of a working through. This is the place of lost bodies and the drowned.

Mantle and lost bodies: a kind of making

In previous art making I have worked with the psychoanalytical structure of trauma. The characteristics of trauma include disturbance of memory, disrupted temporality and refererentiality encapsulated by the term 'afterwardness.' This term is employed by the psychoanalyst Jean Laplanche to describe the peculiar temporality of trauma; how it disrupts linear notions of history and memory, a 'before' and 'after.' Laplanche is of value here not least because he likens the role of transference to what may occur outside the realm of Psychoanalysis, indicating that transference can also take place within the production, transmission and reception of art. His reconfiguration of Freud's 'thing presentation' and 'word presentation' lead ways towards thinking the work of

Section One – Pleasure and Fear in Interdisciplinary Arts Practice

Untitled, Victorian mourning brooch.
(Image: Jane Calow)

mnemic traces that can find channels through to imaging and representation. Unlike Freud and Lacan, Laplanche and Anzieu indicate the importance of sensation outside language, both written and spoken. My working method has been driven by enquiry, thinking the purpose of art making and its contribution to understanding the world and personal investment within it; within my practice this is the crux of the matter. I have found myself snagged upon the horns of a dilemma: how, with a reluctance (on ethical grounds), to render — to 'confess' — what the particularities of traumatic experience might be, yet still persist in working with it, through the conduit of art, thinking and making. Many academics within a number of disciplines, demonstrating varying degrees of success, have attempted to place autobiography within an assortment of theoretical contexts. The 1980s saw the emergence of the term Post-Traumatic Stress Disorder.[5] This included defining the circumstances under which trauma is experienced and I would like to emphasise here, while acknowledging commonality of structuration, how this plays out differently within particular categories of experienced trauma. There is no space here for any extensive elucidation; nevertheless, I feel that markers can be indicated. This is with interlinked aims: the consideration of what may or may not find a way through to some form of representation (including my artistic practice and the place of interdisciplinarity as integral to its theoretical underpinning) and a methodological approach to making.

Fear and Displacements: negotiating being all at sea

My problem for a number of years has been to consider how to produce an artistic practice that eschews and questions expressionism and confession; a practice drawn away from an 'I' yet returns to a narrative of being that cannot ignore the far and near — to consider what to disclose and what is private:

> ...all the while you thought you were going around idle, terribly hard work was taking place. Hard, hard work, excavation and digging, mining, moling through tunnels, heaving, pushing, moving rock, working, working, working, working, panting, hauling, hoisting. And none of this work is seen from the outside. It's internally done.[6]

What is striking about this quotation from the novel by Saul Bellow that begins the text by Graham Ingham, about a trauma patient, is how Ingham identifies processes that may be connected; labour at the level of the unconscious, a process of working through coupled to creativity. It indicates complex relations between the unconscious and consciousness, lived experience and an experience of making, the matter of latency.

And it is at this point to recall, to return to the matter of lost bodies and of drownings. Freud intimates the possibility of the unconscious of one person working with that of another — as does Laplanche through the inscription of the enigmatic message. What is it to be born into grief and mourning? What is it to live with the haunted stories of lost bodies? I know the possibility that unresolved grief and mourning may be passed on to another generation. Psychoanalyst Nicholas Abraham, in resonance with Freud and Laplanche, has written of the 'phantom', where the repressed phantasy of one generation may haunt another generation. 'The phantom is summoned…at the opportune moment, when it is recognised that a gap was transmitted to the subject.'[7] It acts as a stranger within the subject, the haunting 'bears witness to the dead buried within the other.'[8]

Latency, the enigmatic message, condensation, place, displacement and physical place may be where different encounters converge. I am indebted to the Skippers who so kindly talked to me at Newlyn. Again, it is essential to acknowledge the grace of individuals and communities that have entered into communication along my voyage. To enter into candid discussion about their challenging everyday, their recognition of shared community, peril and loss and to witness the pride in what they live was a privilege.

The construction of *Mantle* is a working through, a hopeful movement towards a requiem: a laying to rest. Mantle is such a wonderful word, embodying geological specificity; where the mantle of the earth breaks through the crust — a touching of stones. It is a surfacing. Touch stone. Mantle is also a shroud associated with death; its placing demands the physicality of a body, a funeral.

Within all of these encounters, dialogues and practices lie enquiry and a will to communicate. It is a drive to try to grasp the subtle complexity of communication via whatever conduit. I am interested in a kind of rapport that might possibly be trapped within the processes of making, which may communicate to others.

Working with the texts of Laplanche and Christopher Bollas[9] has provided a possible knitting of psychic structure grounded within the body to engage with the physicality of the world – a psychic and physical sense of spatialisation. Accordingly, Bollas describes as part of the aesthetic experience a rapport that occurs between maker and encounter with Others, that might possibly touch something that stands beside 'language' – potential other ways of experience and thinking the world.[10] It is to the diversity of languages that seek to articulate encounter with the world that I have recourse. It is to the languages of struggle for referentiality that I return. It is to move towards poetics that may touch upon latency, condensations, displacements. Here are extracts from the Bremen Speech by Paul Celan in 1958:

> Within reach, close and not lost, there remained, in the midst of losses,
> This one thing: language.
> This, the language, was not lost but remained, yes in spite of everything.
> But it had to pass through its own answerlessness, pass through a frightful falling mute...
> In this language I have sought, then and in years since then, to write poems - so as to speak, to orient myself, to explore where I was and was
> Meant to go, to sketch out reality for myself.
> It was as you see, event, movement, a being underway, it was an attempt to gain direction. And if I enquire into its meaning, I believe I must tell myself that this question also involves the question of the clock hand's direction.

Through collision of languages in encounter with the world it is to find rapport with Celan. It is to place a message in a bottle, sent out 'towards something standing open.'[11]

Standing on the shore, thinking being, listening to the waves rattle across pebbles.

[1] S. Hall, 'Cultural Studies and the Centre: some problematics and problems', in *Culture, Media, Language*, S. Hall et al (eds), Unwin Hyman Ltd, London, 1990, p. 16.

[2] My previous artwork *Traject* explored the idea of a 'moveable site' through an artist's book and the conversion of seismic data into music, highlighting themes of spatialisation and displacement.

Traject: a way, or a place of crossing over.

A passage or transmission through any medium, or through space.

Vision may be considered...as it signifies the passing or trajection of rays of light.

A perception transmitted to the mind, an impression, a mental picture.

[3] J. Laplanche and J.B. Pontalis, *The Language of Psychoanalysis*, Karnac Books, London, 1988, p. 62.

[4] D. Anzieu, *A Skin for Thought*, Karnac Books, London and New York, 1990.

[5] The definition of Post-Traumatic Stress Disorder appeared in the *Diagnostic and Statistical Manual of Mental Disorders* in America in 1980, largely predicated upon the post-war experiences of Vietnam veterans, but also the experience of victims of child sexual abuse and domestic violence.

[6] Quoted from S. Bellow, *The Adventures of Augie March*, 1953, Penguin Books, London, 1994, in G. Ingham, 'Mental Work in a Trauma Patient' in *Understanding Trauma: A Psychoanalytical Approach*, C. Garland (ed), Gerald Duckworth & Co. Ltd, London, 1998, p. 96.

[7] N. Abraham in *The Shell and the Kernel*, N.T. Rand (ed), The University of Chicago Press, Chicago, London, 1994, p. 174.

[8] Abraham, p. 75.

[9] C. Bollas, *The Shadow of the Object: Psychoanalysis and the Unthought Known*, Free Association Books, London, 1987, p. 32.

[10] Bollas p. 32.

[11] P. Celan. Speech on the occasion of receiving the Literature Prize of the Free, Hanseatic City of Bremen, 1958.

Section Two

— Mutuality — Collaboration and Interdisciplinary Arts Practice

Betwixt and between: prefix, metaphor and performance

– Mike Pearson

Performance Studies regards itself as the quintessentially interdisciplinary discipline. It emerged in the early 1970s in dialogues *between* experimental theatre practice and anthropology. But when Richard Schechner, one of its founding voices, casts it as already and forever *inter* – 'Accepting "inter" means opposing the establishment of any single system of knowledge, values, or subject matter'[1] – he leaves it with a potential crisis of identity. Does it possess an autonomous or singular epistemology or is performance simply a transferable means of 'going on', a 'turn' in discourse? Where can it situate itself politically or ethically in order to act as advocate; from whence does it come and what does it bring to moments of disciplinary encounter and exchange? Forever adrift in a 'no man's land', it is equally prone to forming provisional attachments and alliances and to the risk of being appropriated, or to adopting fashionable re-dressing: the ghost of cultural studies hovers.

Unaligned, nimble, profligate, it may assume the licence to speak on any issue, cognate or otherwise. The recent series of volumes *Theatre &* [everything else] demonstrate this ambition and facility:

> ...over the past fifty years, theatre and performance have been deployed as key metaphors and practices with which to rethink gender, economics, war, language, the fine arts, culture and one's sense of self. *Theatre &* is a long series of short books which hopes to capture the restless interdisciplinary energy of theatre and performance. Each book explores connections between some aspect of the wider world, asking how the theatre might illuminate the world and how the world might illuminate the theatre.[2]

Section Two – Mutuality – Collaboration and Interdisciplinary Arts Practice

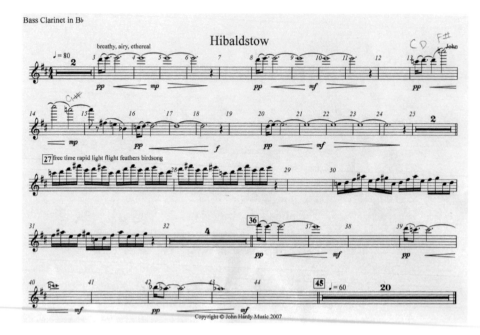

Score for Mike Pearson/John
Hardy *Carrlands*, 2007.

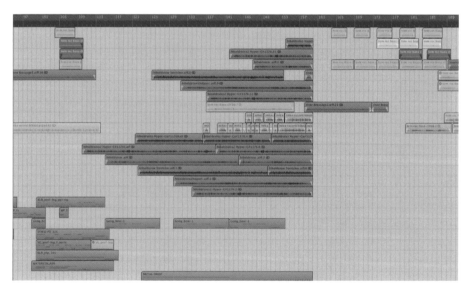

Sound mix for Mike Pearson/John
Hardy *Carrlands*, 2007.

The 'and' is open – it might lead anywhere – though it might indicate a certain assumed primacy: 'theatre &' rather than '& theatre'; theatre can adopt here any guise or position. But 'and' is relatively weak on commitment. What disciplinary borrowings, appropriations and articulations are implied, revealed, or disguised then in the ubiquitous use of *inter*? What happens in meetings of disciplines – discrete, ostensibly dissimilar – areas of scholarly endeavour, rather than in the drawing together of genres of artistic expression in multi-media expositions?

First, it may be necessary to identify what constitute the 'discrete sets of skills or knowledges' of performance and performance studies: to elucidate what it knows about and how it knows it; and how it knows itself and what it knows of itself. This surely entails *intra*-disciplinary reconciliations; the development of projects – 'within' or 'inside' – such as Heike Roms's study of performance art in Wales[3] that resolve history, methodology and theory. To distinguish performance as both mode of enquiry and exposition: as critical optic, theoretical trope, research methodology, creative practice, embodied engagement, and form of representation – as experiencing, knowing and imagining – distinctly, simultaneously. One object may be to determine its terminology, acknowledging inflections of the artistically generic – rhythm, image, composition – whilst recovering the – albeit coined – particularities of performance practice: 'The *sats* [a neologism] is the moment in which the action is thought/acted by the entire organism, which reacts with tensions, even in immobility.'[4]

Then to the prefix, precisely: and here an immediate cause of confusion. *Inter* has two essential meanings: 'between' or 'among' (international); and 'together'. Both include strong implications of *mutual* (interdependent) and *reciprocal* (interpersonal) commitments: both parties are potentially actants, and both may feel the impact of the encounter. But in an *inter*-disciplinary meeting – in the establishment of a middle or common ground – there may be twin hazards: a loss of mutuality in the ceding, forfeiting or diluting of specificities in order to regard jointly or commonly. Can you see what/how I see? And a loss in reciprocity as the one seeks to instrumentalise the other: regarding performance as a purely explanatory device for instance, to explain climate change to schoolchildren. Further, the middle ground may eliminate difference: when for instance disciplines find solace in generic understandings of critical theory, or in applications of digital technology.

There is a signal need for *projects* – locales for 'fruitful dialogue' – within which distinct and differentiated responses to questions are feasible and elicited, and within which disciplinary *inter*sections and articulations are manifest. These might include pre-existing commonalities of interest – in themes, objects and contexts: landscape and environment as arena of contemporary concern and of historical formulation; as field of research and site of artistic endeavour; as medium for and scene of expression. Or in methods of enquiry such as *fieldwork*, within which there are particular disciplinary traditions and understandings of open-air research, observation and mapping, around which collaboration might commence:[5] to be 'afield' together without all becoming either amateur topographers or tourists. With performance as a vital means of embodied engagement...

Following a field workshop of the 'Living in a Material World: Landscapes of Emptiness' network,[6] Angela Piccini asked these questions of the participants, including geographers, artists, performers, archaeologists:

> What is the direction behind the enquiries you made of the site? Is there an agenda – in terms of pedagogy, ideology, practice or philosophy – behind what you set out to do there? What do you believe in (in terms of why you investigate such sites in the way you do)?

In a preparatory field trip for *Warplands*[7] – a 60-minute, multi-media performance of text, soundtrack and projection evoking the landscapes at the mouth of the river Trent – I asked a similar assembly:

> From various disciplinary positions, at various locations: How do you look here and what do you see? How do you get your eye in? What questions do you ask at and about a place like this? What disciplinary optics and approaches are in play? How do you encounter and engage with it? How might you remember and record it? How would you represent or tell about it elsewhere?

Hibaldstow Carrs: Mike Pearson/John Hardy *Carrlands*, 2007
(photo: Mike Pearson).

Alkborough turf maze: AHRC Landscape and Environment programme
'Performing Geographies' workshop, June 2011 (photo: Lucy Veale).

'The emptiest place in Britain': AHRC Landscape and Environment programme
'Performing Geographies' workshop, June 2011 (photo: Lucy Veale).

Geographer Stephen Daniels added:

> What difference does a performative dimension make to researching landscape and environment? Is performance helping us to engage in wider landscape issues effectively? How does performance work with other perspectives on landscape and environment? How does performance help with public value and engagement? How does performance inform and shape narratives of landscape and environment?

And me finally:

> What are potential collective strategies of remembering? How might the experience be developed in interdisciplinary projects of exposition?
> Develop two dramaturgical ideas that may involve text, event and object: as an intervention at site; to reproduce the experience elsewhere.

What *trans*fers? In preparing the form and content of *Carrlands*[8] – a three-hour, web-based audio tour of agricultural landscapes in north Lincolnshire combining text and especially composed soundtrack – I organised a number of field visits with local experts and academic researchers. It was archaeologist John Barrett's perception – that as visitors to heritage sites, our threshold for data retention is surprisingly low and that overload increasingly frustrates us and eventually sullies the experience – that informed the attitudes enshrined in the work. Barrett favours equipping the visitor with tools for interpretation – 'ways of seeing' – rather than lists of dates and periods of building. And from cultural geographers came interest in anthropologist Kathleen Stewart's admonitions[9] in the field to 'Picture this', 'Consider this'; 'Imagine this'...Here the disciplinary relationships are *pedagogical*, from the one to the other.

In *Theatre/Archaeology: Disciplinary Dialogues*[10] – 'a complex interpenetration of the two discourses in an account of projects which begin to fuse performance and archaeology in the dynamic interpretation of the material past.'[11] – Michael Shanks and I outline three broad articulations of the disciplines: theatre archaeology; theatre and archaeology and theatre/archaeology. An 'evolving dialogue between – and the gradual convergence and co-mingling of – two discrete projects: in performance and in archaeology.'[12] Again a relatively supine 'and' but heading we supposed towards 'a blurred genre: a mixture of narration and scientific practices, and integrated approach to recording, writing and illustrating the material past.'[13] The work of articulation would be done in the slash, without the nature of the relationship being prefigured. But even in this developing elision, the two authorial voices – individual perceptions – are distinguished by the use of different typographic fonts.

In describing disciplinary meetings, we seem drawn to prefixes emergent from the realm of the Latin prepositional *accusative* – *in*, *inter*, *trans* – that frequently indicate mobility: direction, movement, motion into, *ad*venture, *in*vasion. Kastner and Wallis's typology of land art[14] is illustrative, as the artist/ agent in various ways moves towards the relatively passive material: *interruption* – employing non-indigenous, man-made materials in intersections of environment and human activity. But what potentials for engagement are additionally revealed through disciplinary encounters in terms prefixed with *circum* – around; *clam* – unknown to; *extra* – outside; *ob* – in front of; *juxta* – close to; *penes* – in the power of; *per* – through; *sub* – under; *ultra* – beyond; *usque* – right up to; *versus* – towards...

Or those deriving from the prepositional *ablative*, often implying position: *cum* – with; *palam/coram* – in presence of; *procul* – far from; *pro* – on behalf of; *simul* – together with; *sub* – under; *prae* – in front of...All manner of possible relativities...

What performance most often seeks in other disciplines are terms and procedures to adequately describe its own practices and processes – *metaphor*: 'a particular set of linguistic processes whereby aspects of one object are 'carried over' or transferred to another object, so that the second object is spoken of as if it were the first'[15]; 'with the aim of achieving a new, wider, 'special' or more precise meaning.'[16] 'Method acting' finds its descriptions in psychology; performance studies initially in anthropology. Often this involves *simile* – the application of a frequently limited analogy or comparison 'like' or 'as if'; though theatre itself is both metonymic – standing in place of – and synecdochic – the substitution of part for whole – in its reflection of everyday life, and indeed essentially simile if, as Schechner suggests, performance is 'restored' or 'twice behaved': 'physical, verbal, or virtual actions that are not-for-the-first-time.'[17]

And what other disciplines seek in performance too is metaphor: from J. L Austin's 'speech acts' to Judith Butler's

Blacktoft: AHRC Landscape and Environment programme
'Performing Geographies' workshop, June 2011
(photo: Iain Biggs)

formulation of 'performativity' via Erving Goffman's anachronistic understanding of theatre to describe the public realm.

Perhaps it is this joint search that attracts performance and other disciplines into a middle ground.

But metaphor is never a perfect fit:

> ...although metaphor undoubtedly deals in likeness, similarity, it also deals in unlikeness and dissimilarity. Metaphor makes us look at the world afresh, but it often does so by challenging our notions of the similarity that exists between things: how alike they are; and in what ways, in fact, they are irreconcilably unalike.[18]

So the imprecision of metaphor might enable us to recognise the detail of our own practices more precisely. For example, what might be revealed in employing geology to dramatic form. In *Site-Specific Performance*[19] dramaturgy is figured conceptually as a *stratigraphy* of discrete layers — text, action, action, soundtrack, technology — each with distinctive (lithographic) features, and from time to time of varying relative thicknesses. Of course, they are not the result of periodic sedimentation and sequential deposition but each 'exposure' — or production — may be susceptible to tilting, folding, faulting and may include erosions and unconformities. And its profile may be subject to sudden, pragmatic *igneous* intrusions of dissimiliar material; or to varied and intense *metamorphic* experiences — of editing, intensification and reassessment — that completely change their initial nature.

So, in the constitution of *Carrlands*:

> The recorded text forms a single layer within a sonic stratigraphy in which separate elements are assigned parallel horizons.
>
> It includes instrumental, vocal and orchestral, and electronic and processed strands; sampling from archival sources — Percy Grainger's folk-song recordings, the voices of Italian prisoners of war; and effects that recall former sound-worlds in these places. And within the matrix, the highly modified, unrecognisable voices of interviewees provide musical textures; or digitally analysed, the notation for instrumental composition itself. The geological analogy is apposite as the sequence is not necessarily even-bedded, and may exhibit folding, faulting and discontinuity. Efficacy is finally assured

through the process of mixing, of relative re-balancing, and even erasure. Become part of a landscape...[20]

And from performance to cultural geography? Of *Carrlands*:

In an essentially expressive rather than explanatory mode, performance can assemble and order material of diverse origins: from the biographical to the bureaucratic. The resulting *dramaturgy* can effect dynamic articulations, jumps, ruptures, elisions, asides, non-sequiturs, illogicalities, circularities and repetitions. Performance can render miscellaneous materials – from the anecdotal to the informational – to the same order of significance; and this it does without need of citation or footnotes. Its rhetorical devices facilitate shifts in viewpoint, attitude and emphasis. Performance deals well with accounts of people and events: it can build *dramos* out of mundane sets of circumstance, and summon sites to emplace them.

...it can draw together narratives, data sets and disciplinary perceptions, both like and markedly unlike; in their juxtaposition, overlay and friction at a certain place, they might reveal its multi-temporality, and through disciplinary convergences, enhance its appreciation.[21]

In *Carrlands*, performance structures include and juxtapose rapidly shifting texts, derived from a variety of disciplinary approaches and in a variety of voices – personal, expert and popular – set within a musical matrix, to reveal better the *imbricated* nature of landscape: favouring local and accented observation and opinion, whilst espousing combinations of the creative and the scientific, the aesthetic and the scholarly. In a participatory, perambulatory work requiring the corporeal involvement of participants and involving an intersection of scholarly and artistic practices – in which interpretation is informed but not monopolised – performance then provides agency without forfeiting its own nature. It provides a methodology or mechanism for examining and enacting the intimate connection between personal biography and the biography of landscape, between social identities and a sense of place, through juxtaposing popular observation with critical academic discourse: in attending to, and accounting of, the nature of places. In apprehensions variously *accusative* and *ablative*...

[1] R. Schechner, *Performance Studies: An Introduction*, Routledge, London, 2002, p. 22.

[2] J. Harvie & D, Rebellato, in *theatre & nation*, N. Holdsworth, Palgrave Macmillan, Basingstoke, 2010, pp. vii-viii.

[3] H. Roms, 'It was forty years ago today...': Locating the early history of performance art in Wales 1965-1979, 2011, viewed on 22 May 2011, <http://www.performance-wales.org>

[4] E. Barba, *The Paper Canoe: a Guide to Theatre Anthropology*, Routledge, London, 1995, p. 55.

[5] S. Daniels, M. Pearson & H. Roms, 'Editorial', *Performance Research*, vol. 15, no. 4, December 2010, p. 1.

[6] A. Piccini, *Living in a Material World: Performativities of Emptiness*, AHRC Landscape and Environment Network, Workshop 1 Bristol Temple Meads, 10-12 October 2006, viewed on 23 May 2011, <http://www.landscape.ac.uk/research/networksworkshops/living_in_a_material_world.htm>

[7] M. Pearson & J. Hardy, *Warplands*, Royal Geographical Society, London, 1 September 2011.

[8] M. Pearson & J. Hardy, *Carrlands*, 2007, viewed on 22 May 2011, <http://www.carrlands.org.uk>

[9] K. Stewart, *A Space on the Side of the Road*, Princeton University Press, Princeton, 1996, pp. 9-10.

[10] M. Pearson & M. Shanks, *Theatre/Archaeology*, Routledge, London, 2001.

[11] Pearson & Shanks, p. 1.

[12] Pearson & Shanks, p. XI.

[13] Pearson & Shanks, p. XI.

[14] J. Kastner & B. Wallis, *Land and Environmental Art*, Phaidon, London, 1998.

[15] T. Hawkes, *Metaphor*, Methuen, London, 1972, p. 1.

[16] Hawkes, p. 2.

[17] Schechner, pp. 34-6.

[18] D. Punter, *Metaphor*, Routledge, London, 2007, p. 9.

[19] M. Pearson, *Site-Specific Performance*, Palgrave Macmillan, Basingstoke, 2010, pp. 166-70.

[20] M. Pearson, 'Deserted places, remote voices: performing landscape', in *Envisioning Landscapes, Making Worlds: Geography and the Humanities*, S. Daniels et al. (eds.) Routledge, New York, 2011, pp. 280-6.

[21] D. Matless & M. Pearson. 'A Regional Conversation', *Cultural Geographies in Practice*, vol 19, January 2012, pp. 123-129.

My thanks are due to my colleagues Dr Carl Lavery and Dr Heike Roms for their critical readings of drafts of this chapter.

You may ask yourself, well, how did I get here?[1]

– Daniel Hinchcliffe

You may ask yourself, well, how did I get here? — Daniel Hinchcliffe

Interdisciplinary study represents, above all, a denaturalization of knowledge: it means that people working within established modes of thought have to be permanently aware of the intellectual and institutional constraints within which they are working, and open to different ways of structuring and representing their knowledge of the world.[2]

Joe Moran feels that interdisciplinary practice challenges certain assumptions that appear to endorse or 'reflect' a construct of a presumed 'natural' order of things. Interdisciplinarity can help us see better how the pressures and limits applied by institutional contexts have effected (or constructed) ways of studying. The very act of entering into interdisciplinary work draws power relations to the surface; quoting Bill Readings, Moran points out that '...attempts at interdisciplinary collaboration are always compromised by their institutional context...'[3] When it works, interdisciplinarity has the potential to enable collaborators to stand back from their own disciplinary bubbles, question practice and have empathy for other world views.

As representational practices, the arts seem particularly appropriate as disciplines with which other areas of study might collaborate to formulate new ways to structure and represent knowledge for new audiences and constituencies. Moran suggests the positive potential of interdisciplinarity as a critical tool that can 'denaturalise' and question received knowledge. At the same time, individuals involved in interdisciplinary processes can find themselves dealing with anxieties around where they or their collaborators belong in the disciplinary landscape. After all, as well as 'making something 'unnatural'', 'denaturalisation' is a term often associated with depriving someone of the rights and privileges of citizenship or of naturalisation. These geographic and migrational overtones seem highly appropriate considering

Section Two — Mutuality — Collaboration and Interdisciplinary Arts Practice

Traject, by Jane Calow.
photograph © Jane Calow

Traject, by Jane Calow.
photograph © Jane Calow

the territorial struggles (both material and metaphorical) that take place interdepartmentally and interpersonally within institutions.

I want to map some of the strategic opportunities – as well as the institutional and intellectual constraints – presented during the history of my artistic/curatorial practice. My practice is driven by a wish to enquire, that has led from making socially invested and often collaborative visual art outside traditional artistic contexts, to curating (often interdisciplinary) art projects and exhibitions in a 'non-arts' higher education institution.

Historical Foundations

I became involved in site-specific art, engaging with location-specific constituencies by the second year of my fine art degree. During the 1980s, choosing to pursue such activities was often construed as part of a critique of the gallery system. Collaborating with other students on artwork caused consternation and conflict amongst fine art teaching staff. Not only did collaboration fly in the face of modernist individualism, but lecturers could not comprehend how they might allocate grading for individual students involved in a group project. During assessment, the marking process became an ideological battlefield between the minority of staff who encouraged students to collaborate and those who felt collaboration posed a threat to artistic 'self-expression'. The same 'modernist' lecturers often felt that work produced in consultation with a place-specific group of non-artists constituted a form of compromise potentially sullying notions of 'pure' self expression (likening the production to 'commercial art' for a 'client' rather than 'fine art'). After graduating I undertook site-specific commissions, artist's residencies, and participatory projects with a range of organisations, groups and individuals. During this period I began teaching at the University of Wolverhampton on the *Fine Art as Social Practice* degree (FASP)[4]. This half theory and half practice course took full advantage of an institution-wide modular system allowing students to combine their study of contemporary fine art practice with disciplines from across the University. The emphasis was on ideas-led contextualised practice, issue-based work, conceptual art and site-specificity. At the time, the CPN (Contextual Practices Network) was a web of Higher Education courses and programmes in Art and Design specifically addressing contextual practice in a way which was at odds with what might be called 'mainstream' art education.[5]

In a climate of increasing marketisation and aggressive competition the CPN promoted mutual support, dialogue and discourse between staff from different institutions. Even for some fellow members of the CPN, the FASP model was challenging in not only combining degrees in anything – from Chemistry to English with Fine Art, but also by encouraging students to bring their other subjects into their art modules. Some outside the course were anxious that undergraduate level was too early to introduce this kind of interdisciplinarity along with a high level of theory.

While at Wolverhampton I completed a PhD exploring collaboration and partnerships in public art commissioning as part of central-business-district-oriented urban regeneration in Birmingham. This included an analysis of how neo-conservative values can manifest themselves in public art schemes produced as part of regeneration aimed at attracting footloose international business investment.

In November 1999 I took up a new Visual Arts post at the University of Bath, a top UK research institution, primarily science and technology-based with no academic arts courses. I joined the staff of the Creative Arts Department, which at that point, in visual arts, primarily provided extra-curricular leisure courses on campus for students, staff and members of the public[6]. There were some dedicated studio spaces; a lecture theatre was available for performances when not in use for academic teaching – and at first there were no formal exhibition spaces. Before long, working with colleagues, I established a programme of professional visual arts exhibitions, talks, symposia and residencies – running alongside music and theatre programmes organised by art form specialists in those areas. In August 2003 the department became the Institute of Contemporary Interdisciplinary Arts (ICIA).

The Politics of Interdisciplinary Collaboration

In Higher Education, enquiry is supposedly paramount, disciplines are clearly defined and the majority of local constituents whether staff or students, have a personal specialist affiliation to a specific academic area. This set of conditions would seem perfect for creating dialogue and interaction between groups and individuals to explore the potential for producing interdisciplinary work. However, there can be a culture of competition between disciplines, departments and individuals over resources.

You may ask yourself, well, how did I get here? — Daniel Hinchcliffe

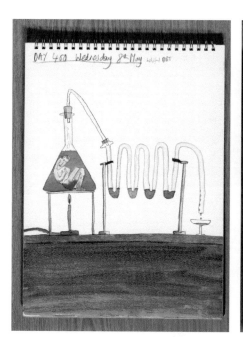

Day 400, by Bobby Baker,
Image © Bobby Baker;
photograph © Andrew Whittuck

Day 584, by Bobby Baker,
Image © Bobby Baker;
photograph © Andrew Whittuck

Margareta Kern, *Guest with Student Halls of Residence Domestic Assistants Wattana and Malgorzata*, 2010.
Photo by: Owen Bryant

Margareta Kern, *Guest with Nano Fab Lab Researchers Steve and Ying Ying*, 2010.
Photo by: Owen Bryant

You may ask yourself, well, how did I get here? — Daniel Hinchcliffe

Margareta Kern, *GUEST*, 2010.
Photo by: Marcus Kern / Post-production: Basia Hrymowicz

Defending academic turf can become an 'art' in itself as David Reason states:

> ...disciplines cannot be politically neutral because they constitute forums within which the competition for resources is fought out, the terms of that battle in the arts as in the sciences being articulated in relation to conceptions of reputation and prestige. Consequently, the traditional disciplines (which date from no earlier than the late 19th century) have an inescapably political or quasi-political character. They organise, advance, secure and embody social and cognitive interests.[7]

Joe Moran sites Roland Barthes' suggestion that interdisciplinarity can question the whole notion of academic specialisation and the tendency of Universities to isolate themselves from the exterior world in 'enclaves of expertise'. Interdisciplinary methods frequently highlight, 'the fact that what is studied and taught within universities is always a political question.'[8]

It has never occurred to some academics that any of the arts might qualify as academic disciplines, or be associated with professionalism. These attitudes are quite innocently held by some individuals who have never previously encountered professional arts practitioners. However, when approached, academics can often be open to learning more about the complexity of what contemporary artistic practice involves and the potential for mutually beneficial interdisciplinary collaboration. Others are actively resistant to the idea that the arts might be worthy of academic or professional status, seeing them as an additional set of potential competitors for resources.

Curating Collaboration – Building

I helped artists to negotiate the internal borders within the University's lived and physical terrain. This can save the artist an enormous amount of time in gaining an overview and a foothold in the context they are entering. I was there to discuss the best way to work with the institution and to get the most out of its organisational features and idiosyncrasies while working with inevitably finite finances, time and resources. This involved pointing out the opportunities, as well as limitations.

Considering the general workload and time pressures weighing upon academics, administrators and students, an institutionally 'embedded' curatorial figure can play an invaluable role in establishing artists' residencies within academic departments; facilitating initial dialogue, building a sense of trust and supporting all involved. As Verwoert states, 'To curate means to talk things into being, not just exhibitions or events but the very social relations out of which such manifestations emerge'.[9]

One key role was to explain to departmental Heads the mutual benefits of collaboration, showing examples of the artist's previous work and indicating the serious level of engagement that would ensue. I made clear that this would be much more sophisticated than a simple 'profile-raising' exercise, and at the same time there would indeed be prestige and press coverage attached to the project. The message was received more readily coming from me as a University member of staff than if a lone artist approached a department from outside. Persuasion became easier as more successful projects and exhibitions were installed at the heart of the campus and became a talking point through the University community.

Over time a sense of anticipation amongst the campus community developed. My strategic approach was to nurture the expectation that a regularly changing selection of ideas-led contemporary art of an unpredictable nature would be encountered in specific locations on campus. It may seem paradoxical, but if people can be encouraged to anticipate the unexpected, the whole interaction with art can have a head start. Through regular encounters with exhibitions of work produced during departmental residencies, academics became familiar with the notion of artists-in-residence as part of campus life. The reception from departmental Heads when approached with proposals to bring artists into their department became progressively warmer and they began making unsolicited requests to host artists.

Prior to running residencies the first thing was to establish regular art shows on campus in places where they couldn't be missed. For my first exhibition programme I constructed a temporary 20-foot square, 8-foot high freestanding gallery space in the middle of the staff common room. Installed over a weekend it appeared unannounced on a Monday morning, and disappeared just as suddenly after two exhibitions. Next, another gallery area was established in the University library and exhibitions expanded in size spreading from there throughout the floors of the library building. The Threshold Gallery followed; named after its location near the main route onto campus. After a run of six exhibitions the building was demolished to make way for a new Sports Training Village. Exhibitions took place in site-specific locations on campus, in Bath city centre and at other galleries until gradually through further negotiated partnerships — with the Estates Department amongst others — a series of three 'foyer' galleries (Art Spaces 1, 2 and 3) were developed across the University. Other locations such as temporary hoardings continued to be used to site artworks.

Conventional gallery spaces are usually policed by 'invigilators' and locked when unsupervised. The three foyer spaces are accessible from early in the morning until late at night, so conventional gallery 'invigilation' is logistically and financially impossible. Artist Becky Shaw's deployment of herself as the conceptualised figure of 'the Receptionist' (see her chapter) was the only occasion in which any one of the three 'unsecured' foyer spaces came close to being 'invigilated', and only during office hours.

Unsecured space means that working with artists on the material manifestation of their work requires forward planning involving thinking all the ways in which art can be physically vulnerable to occasional and usually inadvertent damage. It cannot be assumed that a multi-disciplinary transitional audience will adopt 'correct' formal gallery-going behaviours upon moving through and using a space for its original purpose; a foyer where waiting, leaning on, and scuffing the walls and indeed the art may ensue. I have always warned artists of these constraints in the very first email invitation to exhibit. In this kind of space curatorial and technical support for the artist is particularly important in order to find solutions in the production or reconfiguration of work that responds specifically to the space.[10] Thousands of people from the campus community have traversed these centrally located galleries. To me — having come from a background of working outside the gallery — an unsecured space has benefits in terms of visibility and engagement over a secure cul-de-sac gallery. Physical openness can embody the spirit in which work may be curated and developed for such spaces. This 'lack of security' echoes the intellectual insecurities sometimes associated with interdisciplinary interaction:

In contrast, the project of interdisciplinarity must stress contingency, vulnerability and corrigibility – a kind of humility. Hence the importance of an understanding which locates these master narratives in their historical habitats, and displays them as changing – not always progressing.[11]

I have always found it interesting to approach ideas that I don't at first understand and may well never completely grasp. As a curator working with artists entering non-arts academic departments one of my roles has been to encourage an atmosphere of what David Reason calls 'corrigibility' – that the work in hand is subject to correction, revision and improvement, based on exchanging ideas and recognising the principle of mutual benefit from the project. This goes with a speculative approach that hopes not to prescribe outcomes too tightly.

As the interdisciplinary identity of ICIA became established, new curatorial staff arrived with interdisciplinarity as a central focus.[12] This allowed for greater cross-art form curatorial collaboration with a developed sense of a curatorial team through devising a yearly programming theme. Therefore if a visual artist was interested in developing their work in the direction of performance or sound I could ask one of my colleagues to be involved and vice-versa. We could also plan projects with an embedded cross-art form approach to interdisciplinarity from the start.

Snapshots

Becky Shaw's residency in the Department of Social and Policy Sciences posed questions about the status and expectations of the 'new space', the artist and her audiences: hers could not have been a better project with which to launch the newly converted Art Space 1 at the heart of the University campus. It is not unusual for staff and students to remain unaware of the bulk of what is happening in most other departments of their own University. Artists act as conduits for dialogues between academics from different disciplines over issues that were previously unidentified as being shared. While most of the projects I curated involved a planned public discussion, a demand for additional dialogues often developed through the course of projects. In the case of Becky's residency, a moment arrived when people who had engaged with her individually throughout the residency were keen to be involved in a broader public debate.

Margareta Kern also undertook a residency in the Department of Social and Policy Sciences. She occupied Art Space 1, en route to the busy University refectory. Over the weeks of her residency people passing through saw Margareta's work-in-progress installation develop and change. Via blackboards, she invited staff and students to write about their working life, meet her for a tea break or be photographed with her in their workplace.

She met academics in the fields of work, welfare, globalisation, poverty, social policy and employment. Margareta explored, compared and contrasted her own artistic methods of enquiry with those used in the sociology of work. Her photographic and video work to date had drawn on documentary portraiture, a process resembling anthropological 'field work'. Margareta's project grew out of an understanding that her artistic methods had similarities to academic researchers' work. Intrigued by the public and private use of space at work, Margareta photographed academics' office doors decorated with a mix of professional notices and personal memorabilia. She met with University staff that wear uniforms or protective clothing, such as physics lab technicians, security staff, postal workers, chefs and cleaners. Margareta upturned the conventional divide between artist or researcher and their subject by stepping in front of the camera herself.[13]

Bringing together groups from different disciplinary backgrounds not only raises questions around language but also expected discipline-specific behaviours. *Traject* was an artwork by visual artist Jane Calow exploring the idea of a 'moveable site' through an artist's book and the conversion of seismic data into music, highlighting themes of spatialisation and displacement. Jane worked with composer and artist Kathy Hinde and Dr Sheila Peacock (School of Earth Sciences, University of Birmingham) on a process that generated music from seismic readings taken from a filled-in underpass/shopping area in Birmingham. The computer programme used to translate the data into music, was specially designed for the project by Computer Scientist, Dr Chris Hinde, (Loughborough University of Technology). The launch event at Bath featured cellist Juliet McCarthy performing nine musical 'interruptions', followed by a discussion with the artist and some of her collaborators. Prior to the performance itself, people who usually attended live music, immediately took their seats and waited for the 'recital'. Those regular attendees of art gallery events milled around with drinks as if at a private view. Scientists who appeared less accustomed to attending arts events looked from one group to the other, unsure of what was expected.

Some artists have revisited ICIA over a number of years. In 2003 I invited performance artist Bobby Baker to speak as part of a one-day symposium entitled *Speculative Strategies: Pleasure and Fear in Interdisciplinary Arts Practice*. It was the first time she spoke publicly about making artworks based on her experience of mental illness. She has said that the day acted as a significant tipping point in her thinking about aspects of her work since then. Subsequently, I invited her to contribute work to mark Mental Health Week on campus in 2006, having been approached by the Student Counselling Service and Students Union. When she explained that she had no work suitable for a gallery space I suggested that her partner, a professional photographer, make photographic prints of a selection of the diary drawings she had been making for several years. The ensuing small exhibition in Bath ultimately became a major exhibition, *Bobby Baker's Diary Drawings: Mental Illness and Me 1997-2008*, at Wellcome Collection, London in 2009. Tanya Steinhauser[14] became part of our on-going working relationship, which included a residency, engagement with academics from different departments and the creation of new work.[15]

Sometimes it helps to create a space for dialogue between colleagues who have worked together for years. At one gathering, aimed at introducing an artist to the department in which they were about to take up residence, a fascinating discussion ensued in which scientists shared their various personal interests and activities in the arts from photography to poetry to music. Many present had been colleagues for years and not known anything about one another's enthusiasms for the arts.

Trust, respect and reciprocity are the vital attitudes required for successful interdisciplinary collaboration that overcomes the inevitable constraints of institutional life. Only then can the key participants recognise and hopefully realise the potential for mutual benefit in a project.

[1] Talking Heads, *Once in a Lifetime*, 1981 (David Byrne, Chris Frantz, Jerry Harrison, Tina Weymouth, Brian Eno), Bleu Disque Music Co., Inc./Index Music, Inc. Adm. By WB Music Corp. ASCAP/E.G. Music Ltd. BMI.

[2] J. Moran, *Interdisciplinarity*, Routledge, London and New York, 2002, p. 187.

[3] J. Moran, p. 187.

[4] Run by Jane Calow (originally *Art for Society* set up by David Bainbridge, a founding member of conceptual art group *Art & Language*)

[5] From 1998-04 I was a member, then Secretary, then Chair of the CPN. For a discussion of the philosophy and structure of the CPN see: J. Calow, 'New Territories for Art Education – Finding New Pathways' in *Out the Bubble: Approaches to Contextual Practice within Fine Art Education*. J. Carson & S. Silver (eds), London Institute/ Central St Martins College of Art and Design and London Arts, London, 2000, p. 105.

[6] I worked with many artists over my time at Bath on the development and diversification of the Visual Arts classes and workshops programme but would like to make special mention of Angie Butler's substantial contribution as Teaching Fellow which included delivery of arts courses, as well as technical and studio management responsibilities.

[7] D. Reason, 'Public Art and Collaboration: An Interdisciplinary Approach' in *The International Public Art Symposium: Context and Collaboration*. Public Art Commissions Agency, Birmingham, 1990, 27 and 28 April, p. 61.

[8] J. Moran, p. 17.

[9] J. Verwoert, 'Control I'm Here' in *Curating and the Educational Turn*, P. O'Neill & M. Wilson (eds), Open Editions/de Appel, London, 2010, p. 24.

[10] I and many of the artists I worked with at Bath felt very lucky to have excellent technical support of the most creative, resourceful and patient kind from Charles Farina (Art Technician), Owen Bryant (Media and IT Designer) and Victoria Wastling (Arts Assistant).

[11] D. Reason, p. 61.

[12] Tanya Steinhauser (curating Theatre and Dance), Clive Radford and later Michael Bassett (curating Music and Sound Art).

[13] <http:www.margaretakern.com> viewed on 12 September 2013

[14] Curating Theatre and Dance.

[15] Bobby Baker and sculptor Charlie Whittuck undertook a research and development residency at ICIA followed by a work-in-progress exhibition. Bobby's research was informed by discussions with the University of Bath's Department of Psychology and the Department of Sports Development and Recreation. The residency was the starting point for a large nationally touring performance project linked to the Cultural Olympiad in 2012; *Mad Gyms and Kitchens*, investigating and critiquing the benefits of exercise and nutrition in the pursuit of ultimate physical and mental wellbeing.

You may ask yourself, well, how did I get here? — Daniel Hinchcliffe

Reception: Two Subjects looking at each other

— Becky Shaw

In 2004 I took up an artist's residency at the University of Bath within the Department of Social and Policy Sciences (SPS). The artwork produced was entitled *Reception* and is the vehicle here for a reflection upon art and collaboration. I chose this work partly because it established a working relationship and dialogue with the editors of this publication, but also because it's the work that most sharply raises the problem of the relationship between artist and 'others'- a matter that for me – does not seem to go away.

I often find myself characterised as an artist who collaborates. This is because I've spent time making work in response to environments, practices and professions, considered different to those of the realms of artists. When invited to write about collaboration, I began, and then stopped, suddenly questioning whether any of what I have produced could be considered collaborative. It is not simply that I doubt whether the work has been collaborative 'enough' to reach some quantity or quality of co-operation. Rather, I realised that work I have made asks questions of the relationship of artist and 'others', rather than seeking collaboration as an aim. With hindsight it seems that *Reception* engaged with a philosophical and practical problem that also will not go away - the knotty issue of subjectivity. It seems timely to explore this here, even though, I acknowledge, this must be a 'grand sweep', given the enormity of the subject and the required brevity of the text.

In *Reception*, the notion of visibility in a 'collaboration' is explored. The work was made in response to SPS, a collaboration with a group of specialists rather than one named individual. In response to spending time with academics, I wanted to consider the public front of intellectual pursuit. In this particular context I aimed to explore how academics create and sustain a kind of visibility, at the same time as examining how art and artists become visible. Of course I didn't know that this was what I wanted to do

Photo: Owen Bryant

until I was there; feeling the problems, misunderstandings and expectations placed upon me; combined with those that I placed upon the social scientists.

The artwork was constructed in a foyer space, publicly accessible but not, until that date, converted to an art space; it was this reconfiguration that became *Reception*. This involved installing conventional gallery display equipment like boarding and spotlights, a hired reception desk, IKEA furniture, borrowed University plants, a commissioned pink neon sign saying *Reception*, and myself, in the persona of 'receptionist' to the artist in residence (also myself). Visitors who wished to meet 'the artist' had to make an appointment through 'the receptionist'. Through daily conversation with passing academics themes of discussion arose; including the place of beauty in art and academia, the need and definition of craftsmanship, and what it is we expect artists to contribute to society. The final work was a text, analysing the experiences of the receptionist in relationship to the work of SPS. The text was given to all who passed through the reception on the last day of the exhibition. Following *Reception* this space continued to be a gallery – but minus plants, reception desk, neon sign and receptionist.

Collaboration in context

Emerging in the 1960s and 70s, amongst a variety of artistic strategies, collaboration arose as a stratagem designed to dismantle the commodification of the art object and notions of individual skill, 'genius' and authority. Critical theorists and artists challenged historical models of practice where the artist was characterised as male, white, Western, and allegedly divorced from any concern with society. Numerous collaborative approaches sought to offer more inclusive models of the artist and to change the dynamic between art and its public.

In a nutshell, this artistic critique arose out of a diverse set of cultural discourses, practices and values, eventually known as postmodernism. In simultaneity, the confluence of social change and developments in critical theory generated a movement that could potentially discredit Western ideals of progress. One of the key problems identified by radical theorists (a gloss) was the centrality of the historic and subsequently universalised configuration of the 'individual', 'self' and emergent 'Subject'- the model of an individual agent that could potentially shape society.

The Enlightenment Ideal was a universal figure who could apply rational thinking to analyse the world and transform society. However, in practice this degree of autonomy was only available to a small part of society (white, male, Western). Theorists like Derrida, Foucault and Lyotard criticised the Subject because its ideal was not available to all, and used this to imply then, that a universal conception of mankind was not possible. Their critiques were enormously influential, contributing to the significance of identity politics in the 1970s, 80s and currently.

In his 2002 text, *The Death of the Subject Explained*, James Heartfield analyses these postmodern manoeuvres and identifies a case of 'throwing the baby out with the bathwater'. While agreeing that subjectivity had not achieved its potential because it only belonged to the few, Heartfield claims that to deconstruct the principles of universality potentially generates a precarious situation. When notions of universality are dismantled, the consequence is an elevation of Self in place of the Subject. The idea of the Subject as a being capable of agency (acting and thinking with independence) together with other agents – becomes jeopardised, potentially leaving society with no vision of common needs or goals; the implication leading to a narrowing in expectation of what humanity may achieve.[1]

Heartfield goes on to describe how, as part of the same cultural shift, Marxian intellectuals critiqued the specialisation of academic activity for its inability to capture the shape of society as a totality.

A contextualisation of the place of collaboration in art practice

Within the impact of this theoretical shift in visual art, collaborative artistic practices like Artists Placement Group serve as a good example of commitment to de-specialisation. APG articulated the 1970s zeitgeist that artists' 'generalist' viewpoints might alter, for the good, the particularist perspective of society, particularly those of corporations. In general, the critical direction of collaboration was to establish communities and dissolve the perception of others as 'Other'.[2]

Without the model of the Subject, Heartfield argues, there are no models to explain the potential dynamic of the individual within a society. Models that appear more egalitarian, as in identity politics or Habermas's 'intersubjective' theories elevate

Photo: Owen Bryant

Photo: Owen Bryant

individual qualities over ideals of agency, so dissolving any possibility of the positive aspects of universality, and diminishing the potential for large scale societal change. Heartfield maps how, instead of subjectivity, we have 'ersatz' subjectivity in the form of the individual self – as seen in the rise of media celebritydom and preoccupation with consumption defined identity.

As it seems that the roots of some artistic collaborations lie in the critique of the Subject and the elevation of specific interest communities, artistic practices may offer potential sites to investigate subjectivity. While art is often assumed to explore the 'self' or the individual, could it not instead, be a place to experiment with the figure of the Subject? Perhaps it has always offered a place to 'test' constructs of subjectivity.

Sites of reception and friction

While being the receptionist, my daily encounters were laden with friction, and I was reminded of Allan Kaprow's perception of artistic practice as a means to touch the social 'meniscus' of other people[3]. Kaprow thought artists should push through accepted norms of social distance, considering that the space between people should be charged and active rather than polite. While in reception there were a number of academics who returned daily, either to try to 'catch me out' being 'the artist' instead of the 'receptionist', or to challenge aspects of the work. Some felt that the work was deliberately negative, denying the University beauty or relief from daily life. Others felt that the work was designed to trick or make fools of the staff – that it was about "taking' rather than giving'[4], about making the University population the subjects of the work ('am I in the picture today?'[5]), or about avoiding responsibility by absenting the artist and making the receptionist speak for her. It seemed that the deliberate fronting of the character of the receptionist rankled University staff; testing their ideas and arguments and becoming actively engaged in debate about aesthetic and intellectual value. Instead of seeking common understanding as is often expected of collaboration, *Reception* framed arguments. This was not intended to be crudely divisive, but rather offered a way of asserting the importance of a collision of views.

During the early stages of the residency, I spent time visiting academics in their offices, and attending meetings, lectures and seminars. Being an artist in an academic department, I was neither inside the department nor outside of it, neither student nor teacher.

Reception turned into a vehicle to capture conflicting opinions about art. *Reception* did not intend to create enemies, or 'us' and 'thems', but the encounters it generated provided the grounds, or even a frame for the struggle towards subjectivity. As Heartfield describes, subjectivity is not a given, it is fought for through persuasion.

The act and metaphor of looking is particularly important to *Reception* – people encounter each other, possibly appraising (an/the/each) other. However, in the role of mediator as 'receptionist' and as the artist the power structure lay with me as author. Contrary to post-colonial writing, in the situation of the 'collaboration resistant' artist, my purpose was not to dismantle the structure or to offer a power-free model, but to find the tools to articulate what is there already and to understand the way the individual shapes and is shaped by an encounter with others.

Into Visibility

It seems that relations fraught with difference are central to *Reception*. I play the role of receptionist, surveying all who enter my/receptionist/artist space, while at the same time becoming the most visible port of call. In *Becoming Public*, Emma Hedditch analyses what it means to 'become visible' as an artist. She writes about the act of being in a public context and called artist:

> ...what does it mean to be present at as many places as possible, just to meet the requirement of public appearance? Visibility, surely, is the necessary condition for any discursive relevance, for identification by this public. However, it is provided that a 'being involved' interlinks with the 'becoming visible' within the structures of mutual availability. And this is a matter of property distribution: Anyone who wants to be seen must be available to the community.[6]

In some ways it is problematic to see visibility/appearance as related to subjectivity, as it is more usually associated with promotion of the Self. Hedditch points out that through an awareness of the artist becoming visible, there must be a public – and therefore what could follow has possible implications for engagement with the constitution of type(s) of community. In contrast to the 1960s drive to dispel the individual in favour of commonality, it could be said that through this type of appearance, where one subjectivity engages with others, a model based on agency is offered.

Kelly Large also scrutinises the way each party is perceived by the other, and how this can be made visible as part of the work. In the work *Me, Myself and I*[7] made at New Art Gallery Walsall, she turns the expectation of the artist's talk on its head by inviting a number of other artists to talk about her. The work explores how the artist appears in public, to a public; so shares much with *Reception*. While not strictly a 'collaboration', *Me, Myself and I* produces and explores many complex working relationships, some of which are fraught with difficulty concerning the pressure of representing an other. In a public interview she says of her working method with others:

> ...so my self-deprecation, as I pick out my faults with humour, enables me to normalize or discharge a situation and so find where I 'fit' and where 'art' fits in each specific context. This is not a literal 'fitting in' which involves adapting oneself to the shape of another; it is rather that the attempt (and often failure) in finding a fit is a critical manoeuvre.[8]

The search for whether art and the artist can 'fit' and the failure to do so is the content of the work that must be made visible rather than being a (usually hidden) by-product of collaboration. In the same text she also describes her initial response to a commission as being: 'what can I do, what do they want me to do and what do I want to do?' In this triumvirate of demand, she deliberately takes on the expectations of others and examines her relationship to them, a careful examination of where her own desires and those of others, fit together. The thoughtful process Large describes examines the very grounds of autonomy and the social forms that an individual, or an individual artist bangs against and is defined by.

Visibility demands recognition by others: to look and to be seen, so this aspiration to explore visibility must be social. However, the visibility that Large, Hedditch and *Reception* explore is also about what it is to form an individual identity in a context. By avoiding assumed models of collectivity and co-operation, is the only other available model of the individual a knee-jerk return to identity politics — is there nothing left of the ideal of the Subject? In her online text, Irit Rogoff, wrote about collaborations that try to look in detail at what happens within the process of collaboration, which can:

> [Emphasize] a critical interrogation of the processes of production through artistic practice, the loss of the so-called autonomy of the work of art, and the subjugation of the heroic individual artist to the cultural embeddedness of the artwork.[9]

As Rogoff intimates, earlier collaborations have offered critiques of the cult of individualism and heroism attached to the idea of 'artist', answering this with the recognition that art is socially produced. However, for artists who have grown up with sequential critiques of individuality: the critique of the white male hero; self-sacrificial models of community practice, and then the packaged models of community in Relational Aesthetics, it seems there are limited models of individuality beyond a biographically driven narrative of Self.

It seems important that artists are given the space to examine what it means to reflect not just on commonality, but also the significance of individuality, to see if an exploration of something more than the Self is possible. It seems that both contrary to, and because of, its history, 'collaboration' provides fruitful grounds to inquire into the terms that attempt to capture subjectivity.

In conclusion, I want to return to an idea of mistaken identity and reflect on those artists who also look like they collaborate but are doing something else altogether. These artists get into close proximity with different professional fields so might easily be mistaken for sharing some of the political motives of earlier collaborative practices. These artists don't share many of the social or ethical imperatives of their ancestors, rather they inhabit a different political context where some of the previous reasons for collaboration are turned upside down.

It seems that contrary to ideals about community or commonality, I (and others) enter social contexts to work out what contemporary subjectivity might be.

[1] J. Heartfield, *The 'Death of the Subject' Explained*, Sheffield Hallam University, Sheffield, 2002.

[2] <wikipedia.org/wiki/Collaboration> viewed on 3 August 2011

[3] A. Kaprow, *Essays on the Blurring of Art and Life*, J. Kelley (ed), University of California Press, Berkeley and Los Angeles, 2003.

[4] B. Shaw, *Reception* essay, hand distributed at University of Bath, 2004.

[5] B. Shaw, *Reception* essay.

[6] K. Meunier and E. Hedditch, 'Appearing, Becoming Visible, Having a Public Face', in *Coming to Have a Public Life: Is it Worth it?* E. Hedditch (ed). Commissioned by Art Now Live, Tate Britain. 2007, p.5.

[7] K. Large, *Me, Myself and I*, New Art Gallery Walsall, 2008.

[8] K. Large and B. Shaw, *Please do not Confront me with my Failures, I have not Forgotten them*, Transmission Chapbook, Artwords Press, London, 2010.

[9] I. Rogoff, *Production Lines. Collaborative Arts*, viewed on 3 August 2011, <http://collaboarts.org/?p=69>

Section Three

— Ethics, Interdisciplinary Arts Practice
and the Politics of Negotiation

The Transitional Space of Interdisciplinarity

— Jane Rendell

In recent times there has been a disturbing sense that the arena of arts and humanities-led interdisciplinary work – grounded in critical, ethical and political debate – is being appropriated and used to deliver instrumental government policy: to answer questions rather than pose them, and to provide market-driven solutions rather than challenge ideological norms. This essay argues for the importance of acknowledging the more relational and thus emotional aspects of interdisciplinary research and practice, suggesting that it is only by paying attention to the psychic dimension of interdisciplinarity that we can understand its transitional status and transformational potential, and so better position ourselves in today's sites of contestation.

In both academic and arts-based contexts, the term interdisciplinarity is often used interchangeably with multidisciplinarity, but I understand the terms to mean quite different things. Multidisciplinarity research for me describes a way of working where a number of disciplines are present but maintain their own distinct identities and ways of doing things; whereas in interdisciplinarity research individuals operate between, across and at the edge of their disciplines and in so doing question the ways in which they usually work. This can occur when one individual's work moves from one discipline to another, and it can also occur when individuals from different disciplines work with one another getting closely engaged in the procedures and ideologies that structure each other's research modes and practice paradigms. Elsewhere I have described the patterning of this kind of work, in terms of critical spatial practices, processes that tend to operate horizontally: surveying a field, examining the fissures, the points where disciplines come apart, the precise nature of the places where they come together – at boundaries, in folds and overlaps, across tears and rips; rather than vertically, where the techniques of in-depth focused research might be favoured.[1]

In exploring questions of method or process that discussions of interdisciplinarity inevitably bring to the fore, Julia Kristeva has argued for the construction of 'a diagonal axis':

> Interdisciplinarity is always a site where expressions of resistance are latent. Many academics are locked within the specificity of their field: that is a fact ... the first obstacle is often linked to individual competence, coupled with a tendency to jealously protect one's own domain. Specialists are often too protective of their own prerogatives, do not actually work with other colleagues, and therefore do not teach their students to construct a diagonal axis in their methodology.[2]

In my view, engaging with this diagonal axis demands that we call into question what we normally take for granted, that we question our methodologies, the way we do things, and our terminologies, the words we give to the things we do. The construction of 'a diagonal axis' is necessarily a difficult business. Kristeva's phrase 'expressions of resistance' points to the unconscious operations at work in interdisciplinary practice.[3] And cultural theorist Homi Bhabha also describes the encounter between disciplines in psychoanalytic terms as an 'ambivalent movement between pedagogical and performative address' – suggesting that we are both attracted by and fearful of the interdisciplinary.[4]

It is precisely for this reason that I am a passionate advocate for interdisciplinarity; because such projects are for me critical, ethical and political but also emotional and unpredictable – interdisciplinary work *is* difficult – not only materially and intellectually, but also psychically. In demanding that we exchange what we know for what we do *not* know, and that we give up the safety of competence and specialism for the fear of inability and the associated dangers of failure, the transformational experience of interdisciplinary work produces a potentially destabilizing engagement with existing power structures, allowing the emergence of fragile forms of new and untested experience, knowledge, and understanding.

Given the recent appropriation of the term interdisciplinarity in the meta-discourses of academe and higher education, where the word is now used in place of multidisciplinarity, it seems important to distinguish the particular qualities of an interdisciplinary approach. I suggest that the aim of such work is to question dominant processes that seek to control intellectual and creative production, and to instead generate new resistant forms of research and practice. In following a desire to imagine rather than apply, to invent rather than to copy, this kind of activity requires emotional as well as mental and physical energy, it therefore needs to be positioned within the context of psychic experience, particularly in connection to different psychoanalytic concepts concerning the transitional processes and subjective spaces of relationality:

The focus of the theory of object relations created and developed by the Independent British Analysts is the unconscious relationship that exists between a subject and his/her objects, both internal and external.[5] D. W. Winnicott introduced the idea of a transitional object, related to, but distinct from, both the external object, the mother's breast, and the internal object, the introjected breast. For Winnicott, the transitional object or the original 'not-me' possession stands for the breast or first object, but the use of symbolism implies the child's ability to make a distinction between fantasy and fact, between internal and external objects.[6]

I have introduced the terms 'transitional object' and 'transitional phenomena' for designation of the intermediate area of experience, between the thumb and the teddy bear, between the oral eroticism and true object-relationship, between primary creative activity and projection of what has already been introjected, between primary unawareness of indebtedness and the acknowledgement of indebtedness.[7]

This ability to keep inner and outer realities separate yet inter-related results in an intermediate area of experience, the 'potential space', which Winnicott claimed is retained and later in life contributes to the intensity of cultural experiences around art and religion.[8] Winnicott discussed cultural experience as located in the 'potential space' between 'the individual and the environment (originally the object)'. In Winnicott's terms, for the baby, this is the place between the 'subjective object and the object objectively perceived'.[9]

This potential space is at the interplay between there being nothing but me and there being objects and phenomena outside omnipotent control. … I have located this important area of *experience* in the potential space between the individual and the environment, that which initially both joins and separates the baby and the mother when the mother's love, displayed as human reliability, does in fact give the baby a sense of trust, or of confidence in the environmental factor.[10]

It is the potential space offered by interdisciplinary work that I believe is such a strong attractor; another, as yet unknown, discipline offers the chance to 'loose control'.[11] And if interdisciplinarity can be defined as the making of relationships between one discipline and another – through subject *and* object relations – then we might argue that the very work of interdisciplinarity is configured around the process of making relationships, continuously confronting the question of what it means to relate to, and therefore recognise, an 'other'. As psychoanalyst Jessica Benjamin writes, this question of 'how is it possible to recognise an other?' has been a key concern of feminism,[12] while in her view the central task of psychoanalysis is the 'double task of recognition: how analyst and patient make known their own subjectivity and recognise the other's'.[13] Benjamin's interest is in pushing beyond reversal, 'by contemplating the difficulty of creating or discovering the space in which it is possible for either subject to recognise the difference of the other'.[14] Grounded in the object relations theory of Winnicott, Benjamin argues that psychoanalysis requires both an intrapsychic focus to examine relations between the self and the internalised other as object, and an intersubjective approach to explore the relationship between subjects and externalised others.[15]

Such a theoretical perspective suggests that objects exist both internally and externally and mediate transitional spaces – moving back and forth in both directions – across and through inner and outer worlds and the places between them. In visual and spatial culture, feminists have drawn extensively on psychoanalytic theory to think through relationships between the spatial politics of internal psychical figures and external cultural geographies.[16] The field of psychoanalysis explores these various thresholds and boundaries between private and public, inner and outer, subject and object, personal and social in terms of a complex understanding of the relationship between 'internal' and 'external' space. Cultural geographer Steve Pile has described it like this:

> While inner life is distinct, there is continuous exchange
> between the internal and external, but this 'dialectic' is
> itself interacting with the transactions between 'introjection'
> and 'projection'.[17]

The psychic processes of recognition and identification,
as well as introjection and projection, provide a rich source of
conceptual tools for exploring the complex relationships made
between subjects and others, and between people, objects and
spaces. Benjamin argues that once we start to think in terms of
relationships between subjects, or subjectivity, we have no choice
but to consider these intrapsychic mechanisms of relation, most
importantly identifications: 'Once subjectivity is embraced',
she says, 'we have entered into a realm of knowledge based on
identifications, hence knowing that is intrapsychically filtered.'[18]

Feminist theorist Diane Fuss also states that identification is
'a question of relation, of self to other, subject to object, inside to
outside';[19] it is, she writes, 'the psychical mechanism that produces
self–recognition'.[20] While Fuss outlines how identification
involves the interrelationship of two processes each working in
different directions: introjection, the internalisation of certain
aspects of the other through self-representation, and projection,
the externalisation of unwanted parts of the self onto the other,
visual theorist Kaja Silverman has explored identification in terms
of cannibalistic or idiopathic identification where one attempts
to absorb and interiorise the other as the self, and heteropathic
identification where 'the subject identifies at a distance' and
in the process of identification goes outside his/herself.[21] This
tension that operates between obscuring and so loosing the
other, and/or being engulfed or lost within the other, is perhaps
the key experience of interdisciplinary work, and its qualities of
imagination and mystery, fantasy and seduction.

Psychoanalyst Jean Laplanche is probably best known for his
re-examination of Sigmund Freud's controversial abandonment of
the seduction theory, and his turn to the child's fantasy to explain
seduction, thus at some level, according to Laplanche, avoiding
thinking-through the complex interplay of inner and outer
worlds between the child and what Laplanche calls 'the concrete
other'.[22] Laplanche maintains that this early scene of seduction
is of key importance to psychoanalysis as it works to de-centre
the position of the subject in its articulation of the formation and
role of the unconscious. For Laplanche, it is the embedding of the

alterity of the mother in the child, which places an 'other' in the subject; this other is also an other to the mother – as it involves her unconscious. Thus, the message imparted to the subject by the other – in Laplanche's writings, the mother or concrete other – is an enigma both to the receiver, but also to the sender of the message: the 'messages are enigmatic because ... [they] are strange to themselves'.[23]

In Laplanche's discussion of the enigmatic message he suggests that transference – or the work of psychoanalysis – occurs not first in the psychoanalytic setting to be applied in culture, but the other way around: 'maybe', he writes, 'transference is already, "in itself", outside the clinic'.[24] For Laplanche, the analyst or recipient subject is involved in a two-way dynamic with the enigmatic message: s/he is, 'caught between two stools: the enigma which is addressed to him, but also the enigma of the one he addresses, his public'.[25]

More recently, Laplanche has supplemented his concept of the enigmatic message with an account of seduction that emphasises the importance of inspiration, or the role of the other as muse.[26] In this investigation Laplanche inverts the traditional model of creative self-expression outlined in Freud's 'Creative Writers and Daydreaming' (1908), arguing that the 'moment of address' should be inverted from its narcissistic aspect, where it moves from the creator's self expression to a receptive public who are expected to provide a beneficial response to the public, whose expectation provokes the creative work: 'it is the public's expectation, itself enigmatic, which is therefore the provocation of the creative work ... '.[27]

In recognising the importance of transference in cultural activities that take place outside the clinic – the potential and often unexplainable resonances produced by the enigmatic and seductive qualities of 'messages': their strangeness, the ways they inspire, the manners in which they excite expectation – the writings of Laplanche are key to conceptualising processes of relation in interdisciplinarity in terms of creativity.[28] It is interesting to consider his understandings of the seductive qualities of the enigmatic other in parallel to Winnicott's notion of transitional space with its qualities of potential-ness as the place of relation between two. The role psychic processes – intrapsychic and intersubjective – including identification, recognition, introjection, projection, transference, seduction and inspiration – play in structuring the complex emotional space of interdisciplinary work, needs to be acknowledged in order to allow us to realise the care and time required to research and practice in this way. In order to generate a culture of mutual respect in these times of appropriation, skills of trust and concern are needed to balance the ever-present more destructive passions, such as jealousy and suspicion, as well as to help work-through the often debilitating aspects of anxiety and ambivalence.

At the moment of writing, government initiatives in higher education are increasingly focusing on financial objectives: on the one hand, the practice of teaching is being pushed towards a phase of deepened alienation – with the acquisition of knowledge valued in solely monetary terms: and on the other, research funding is being directed to favour enterprise and impact – with the commodification of concepts, experiences and emotions, as well as the more obvious object-like artefacts, patents and prototypes, tipped towards their potential sale at the market. In such an atmosphere, the value of arts and humanities research and practice, with its rich history of politically-driven interdisciplinary work is in grave danger of becoming unhinged from its ethical underpinnings and history of critical theory, becoming attached instead to industrial applications and problem-solving agendas. Against our protestations, we are seeing, almost daily, the marginalization of those areas of research and practice that do not demonstrate short-term economic benefit, and the stealthy creep of recuperation: the use of terms which derive from the arts and humanities – such as interdisciplinarity – that stand for critical, ethical and political ways of working – to support non-principled agendas and pragmatic delivery techniques.

When the focus on creativity is driven by 'application', it is less usual for an artist/designer/writer to operate in an interdisciplinary way, to make a 'problematic' artefact that questions the context of application and adopts another discipline's perspective in order to reflect critically on the ideological assumptions which underpin its own methods. As the agenda of UK teaching and research increasingly heads to market we need to protect work that values self-questioning over more positivist models, often self-congratulatory, of short-term implementation and financial benefit. Interestingly, it might be that the very emotional register of interdisciplinary work, which I have argued here lies at the heart of interdisciplinarity, may be a site of potential strength due to its vulnerable nature. In resistance the ability to be subtle, to know how to care for fragility, to be able to make strong relationships as well as critique concepts, practices and methods, may be vital in building alternatives. The ethics of interdisciplinary – the fascination of one for the other – configured as respect for difference, certainly allows for the exploration of boundaries and transitional processes, yet as well as using these abilities to reveal the workings of power in disciplinary structures of knowledge, and exposing strategies of appropriation and recuperation, right now such skills are being put to action in the formation of new social movements. We need these qualities even more urgently today in order to nurture the emergence of these marginal and often complex forms of practice that are at once questioning of dominant ideological and economic systems and capable of constructing relations and proposing futures other than those envisaged for the short-term by neo-liberal capitalists in pursuit of immediate financial gain.

[1] See Jane Rendell, J. Rendell, *Art and Architecture: A Place Between*, IB Tauris, London, 2006, and J. Rendell, *Site-Writing: The Architecture of Art Criticism*, IB Tauris, London, 2010.

[2] J. Kristeva, 'Institutional Interdisciplinarity in Theory and Practice: an interview', in *The Anxiety of Interdisciplinarity, De-, Dis-, Ex-*, vol.2, A. Coles & A. Defert, (eds), Blackdog Publishing, London, 1997, pp. 3-21, pp. 5-6.

[3] See for example J. Benjamin, *Shadow of the Other: Intersubjectivity and Gender in Psychoanalysis*, Routledge, London, 1998, p. 25 and D. Fuss, *Identification Papers*, Routledge, London, 1995, pp. 2-3.

[4] H. K. Bhabha, *The Location of Culture*, Routledge, London, 1994, pp. 163.

[5] G. Kohon (ed.) *The British School of Psychoanalysis: The Independent Tradition*, Free Association Books, London, 1986, p. 20. The British School of Psychoanalysis consists of psychoanalysts belonging to the British Psycho-Analytical Society, within this society are three groups, the Kleinian Group, the 'B' Group (followers of Anna Freud) and the Independent Group.

[6] D. W. Winnicott, 'Transitional Objects and Transitional Phenomena – A Study of the First Not-Me Possession', *International Journal of Psycho-Analysis*, vol. 34, 1953, pp. 89–97, see in particular pp. 89 and 94. See also D. W. Winnicott, 'The Use of an Object', *The International Journal of Psycho-Analysis*, vol. 50, 1969, pp. 711–716.

[7] Winnicott, 'Transitional Objects and Transitional Phenomena', p. 89.

[8] Winnicott discussed cultural experience as located in the 'potential space' between 'the individual and the environment (originally the object)'. In Winnicott's terms, for the baby this is the place between the 'subjective object and the object objectively perceived'. See D. W. Winnicott, 'The Location of Cultural Experience', *The International Journal of Psycho-Analysis*, vol. 48, 1967, pp. 368–372, p. 371. See also D. W. Winnicott, *Playing and Reality*, Routledge, London, 1991.

[9] Winnicott, 'The Location of Cultural Experience', p. 371.

[10] Winnicott, 'The Location of Cultural Experience', pp. 371-2.

[11] For an intelligent and moving account of what it means to loose control in collaborative and interdisciplinary architectural practice see D. Petrescu, 'Losing Control, Keeping Desire', in *Architecture and Participation*, P. Blundell Jones, D. Petrescu & J. Till (eds), Spon Press, London, 2005, pp. 43–64.

[12] Benjamin, *Shadow of the Other*, p. 80.

[13] Benjamin, *Shadow of the Other*, p. xii.

[14] Benjamin, *Shadow of the Other*, p. xii. See also J. Benjamin, 'An Outline of Intersubjectivity: The Development of Recognition', *Psychoanalytic Psychology*, vol. 7, 1990, pp. 33–46, especially pp. 34–35 and J. Benjamin, 'Response to Commentaries by Mitchell and by Butler', *Studies in Gender and Sexuality*, vol. 1, 2000, pp. 291–308, p. 302.

[15] Benjamin, *Shadow of the Other*, p. xiii and p. 90.

[16] See for example, S. Stanford Friedman, *Mappings: Feminism and the Cultural Geographies of Encounter*, Princeton University Press, Princeton, 1998; Fuss, *Identification Papers*; E. Grosz, *Volatile Bodies: Toward a Corporeal Feminism*, Indiana University Press, Bloomington and Indianapolis, 1994; I. Rogoff, *Terra Infirma*, Routledge, London, 2000; and K. Silverman, *The Threshold of the Visible World*, Routledge, London, 1996.

[17] S. Pile, *The Body and The City*, Routledge, London, 1999, p. 91. See also Grosz, *Volatile Bodies*, pp. 27–61.

[18] Benjamin, *Shadow of the Other*, p. 25.

[19] Fuss, *Identification Papers*, p. 3.

[20] Fuss, *Identification Papers*, p. 2.

[21] Silverman, *The Threshold of the Visible World*, pp. 23–24.

[22] C. Caruth, *An Interview with Jean Laplanche*, © 2001 Cathy Caruth, viewed on 3 May 2006. See http://www3.iath.virginia.edu/pmc/text-only/issue.101/11.2caruth.txt Laplanche notes that Freud uses the terms *der Andere* and *das Andere* to distinguish the other person from the other thing. See J. Laplanche, 'The Kent Seminar, 1 May 1990', in *Jean Laplanche: Seduction, Translation and the Drives*, J. Fletcher & M. Stanton (eds), The Institute of Contemporary Arts, London, 1992, pp. 21–40, p. 25.

[23] Caruth, 'An Interview with Jean Laplanche'.

[24] J. Laplanche, 'Transference: its Provocation by the Analyst' [1992] translated by L. Thurston, in *Essays on Otherness*, J. Fletcher, (ed), Routledge, London, 1999, pp. 214–233, p. 222. See also J. Laplanche, *New Foundations for Psychoanalysis*, translated by D. Macey, Basil Blackwell Ltd., Oxford, 1989, pp. 152–154.

[25] Laplanche, 'Transference: its Provocation by the Analyst', p. 224.

[26] J. Laplanche, 'The Theory of Seduction and the Problem of the Other', *International Journal of Psycho-Analysis*, vol. 78, 1997, pp. 653–666, p. 665.

[27] J. Laplanche, 'Sublimation and/or Inspiration', translated by L. Thurston & J. Fletcher, *New Formations*, vol. 48, 2002, pp. 30–50, p. 49. See also S. Freud, 'Creative Writers and Day-Dreaming' [1908], in *The Standard Edition of the Complete Psychological Works of Sigmund Freud, Volume IX (1906–1908): Jensen's 'Gradiva' and Other Works*, translated from the German under the general editorship of J. Strachey, The Hogarth Press, London, 1959, pp. 141–154.

[28] The work of Laplanche has been taken up in film, literary and art history. See R. Rushton, 'The Perversion of The Silence of the Lambs and the Dilemma of The Searchers: on Psychoanalytic "Reading"', *Psychoanalysis, Culture & Society*, vol. 10, no. 3, December 2005, pp. 252-268; A. Stack, 'Culture, Cognition and Jean Laplanche's Enigmatic Signifier', *Theory, Culture & Society*, vol. 22, no. 3, 2005, pp. 63–80 and M. Nixon, 'On the Couch', *October*, vol. 113, Summer 2005, pp. 39–76.

The End of the Road: Oil, Arts Sponsorship and Interdisciplinary Campaigning

— Jane Trowell, Platform

Platform is a London-based interdisciplinary group of artists, activists, researchers and campaigners who work together on issues of social and environmental justice. In this chapter, we explore interdisciplinary practice through examining one current campaign that connects up many issues: the ethics and motivations behind oil company sponsorship of the arts. Vignettes from the campaign will be followed by commentary that draws out issues arising from interdisciplinary ways of working.

It may be true that one has to choose between ethics and aesthetics, but it is no less true that whichever one chooses, one will always find the other at the end of the road. (Jean-Luc Godard, film director)

It's 3rd July 2011 at London's Southbank Centre, (SBC) Britain's biggest arts venue. There are 20 minutes to go before colleagues present our forthcoming book The Oil Road,[1] a poetic, critical travelogue mapping the route and impacts of oil from beneath the Caspian seabed along 5000 km of BP's pipelines and tanker routes to the refineries of central Europe. The event is part of SBC's London Literature Festival, and we're in a room, high up, whose sheet glass windows look out onto the London HQ of oil company Shell. However, the Duty Manager has been called by a concerned member of staff. He's got to look at our reports and leaflets before we can display them on a table for the public's interest. The DM scans the materials and then asks whether there's any about Shell, pointing out that they're a major sponsor of SBC, and that SBC can't display anything critical.

After the event, we email SBC's Artistic Director Jude Kelly and Chief Executive Alan Bishop to challenge this attempted censorship. Jude promptly phones us 'to put something right that is clearly wrong', and explains in an email that SBC has 'no policy at all that instructs staff to avoid criticism of sponsors', and that conversations will be had internally among staff to ensure this doesn't happen again. All very interesting.

From the founding of Platform, back in 1983, we've asserted that society's injustices could not be undone by people working in isolated 'specialisms': ecologists on ecology, human rights campaigners on social justice, politicos on politics, artists on culture etc. In fact, it is our view that societies reach crisis precisely because of the gaps in understanding caused by such a framework. The expert who knows 'ever more about ever less' is a fetish in European-dominated culture, predicated on preserving power. It emerges out of the notion that only elites who have gone through all the educational levels are allowed to think about the big picture.[2] 'Ever more about ever less' can lead to people even in elite positions unable or unwilling to communicate beyond their field or beyond their community's self-interest, so specialised and disciplinary has their knowledge become. Individuals who do speak across cultures, science, politics, communities etc, get hailed as exceptional, elected as leaders, marginalised, banged up, or dismissed as dilettantes depending on whose interests their insights serve or undermine.

A child is not born into the world thinking in 'subjects'. Schooling is what first fosters this splitting. In UK primary schools, interestingly, there is usually one teacher who teaches all 'subjects' and might even integrate them. But it's at secondary school, where the rot sets in in earnest. "I've got history next, what have you got?" as if pupils are afflicted with discrete conditions, ministered to by specialists in discrete rooms, between whom young people travel to receive separate infusions.[3] Despite some schools' attempts at cross-curricularity, at interconnecting issues, as Bernstein says, "we must ask, in whose interest is the apartness of things, and in whose interest is the new togetherness and the new integration?...the long socialisation into the [existing] pedagogical code can remove the danger of the unthinkable and of alternative realities."[4]

The book *The Oil Road* presents an interwoven and deeply human analysis of the impacts of our dependency on oil, gathered from homes, pipeline sites, meetings with oil workers, oil installations, books, websites, and Freedom of Information requests. This material could have resulted in a report but the decision to write it and position it as literature – and the fact it was programmed as such by the Southbank Centre – is one that promotes a systemic and integrated vision that says that aesthetics, ethics and politics are as much the domain of the 'artist' as the 'human rights activist', the 'oil analyst' or any of us. In fact it blurs those very definitions. It says the artist can analyse oil, the human rights activist can write poetically, the oil analyst can be deeply concerned about the environment. The two authors of *The Oil Road* identify as many things — artist, researchers, activists, and the book's style and content aims to reflect this.

SBC invited us to present this work which is both political and aesthetic, yet the event revealed another form of splitting: the Duty Manager's censoring actions which were obvious to him and the Artistic Director's insistence that there was no policy of censorship. The 'need to know' basis that is common in many big institutions (which privileges which person in which role should know which information) cuts down on discussion, and hierarchizes knowledge. It can also lead to anomalies such as a venue hosting an event deeply critical of one oil company while worrying — in the DM's case — about fostering dissent against another whose corporate behaviour is equally under scrutiny.

It's 5.30pm on 18th July 2011 on the ramp at Tate Modern. Reverend Billy and his Church of Earthaluyah Choir, joined by a host of activists and artists, are about to perform a dramatic exorcism to remove BP from being one of Tate's major sponsors. They've come at the request of UK Tar Sands Network (UKTSN), London Rising Tide, Liberate Tate, Art Not Oil, and Climate Rush. These groups support UKTSN which campaigns in partnership with indigenous communities affected by the massive Tar Sands oil developments in Canada. While some police officers had been circling the ramp area before the well-publicised exorcism, neither they nor Tate staff intervene in the intense 15-minute performance. The cameras are rolling after all, and it would be foolish to make a good story even better. One of the performers later explains:

> *When Tate takes money from the fossil fuel industry it is endorsing climate change rather than backing activity which moves us away from an environmental crisis that is already destroying lives and livelihoods. We have to ensure our public arts institutions are financed responsibly, transparently and ethically for the good of the art world and the planet.*[5]

Section Three — Ethics, Interdisciplinary Arts Practice and the Politics of Negotiation

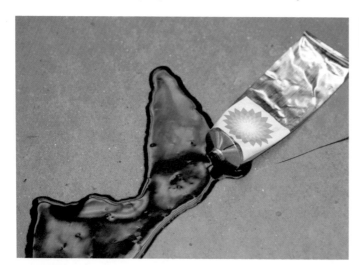

Sunflower (14th September 2010) Oil on Concrete, Liberate Tate; Tate Modern, London. Photo by Jeffrey Blackler

Toni and Bobbi (28th June 2010) Molasses, rubble sacks, strap-on harnesses, floral dresses. Liberate Tate; Tate Summer Party, Tate Britain, London. Photo by Immo Klink.

Licence to Spill (28th June 2010) Molasses, oil cans, feathers. Liberate Tate; Tate Summer Party, celebrating 20 years of BP sponsorship, Tate Britain, London. Photo by Immo Klink

The next day, John Vidal suggests in The Guardian that 'the art establishment is losing the war against the growing movement by activists...What to BP, Shell and the art establishment was, to begin with a mild irritant, is in danger of becoming an open wound.'[6] Two weeks later, over 8000 people have viewed the exorcism on YouTube, the irritant becoming a rash.[7]

Over the past 10-15 years there has been a melting of barriers between those involved in direct action, environmental justice, art and creativity. We see this recently in UK social movements such as Climate Camp, No Borders, Climate Rush, Art Not Oil, UK Uncut, Arts Uncut, Free University movements and Occupy, where the outpourings of visual, text-based, performative and film interventions have successfully involved a wide range of people, dominated the media and grabbed the public's attention. There's a new generation of creative activists who have synthesised media-savviness and the power of the arts, with a strong, well-argued message. It's no longer odd to find artists from all disciplines involved in social movements, NGOs and campaigns, nor activists thinking laterally and creatively about how an action will look, or operate at a visceral level. The 'creative' is valued as much as the need for good footnotes to back up the campaign.

The revival in a culture of teach-ins and skill-sharing that has been fostered through Climate Camp and recent art school occupations is connected to the involvement in these movements of such groups as the Laboratory of Insurrectionary Imagination (Labofii), Corporate Watch and Platform.[8] Labofii's first 'experiment' was at the European Social Forum held in London in 2004, where hundreds of artist-activists gathered in the Rampart Social Centre to meet, discuss capitalism and devise creative interventions and disruptions over the duration of the ESF. Corporate Watch was set up in 1996 as a cooperative. The founders were a group of dynamic activists in their twenties who wanted to support environmental protests by demystifying how corporations work, and providing far more detailed public research and data than was then available. They successfully made the case for spending time on research, and waves of ex-Corporate Watch researchers have infused numerous movements with this attitude. Platform has consistently promoted this way of working since the 1980s through the work itself, but also workshops, courses and publishing. The 36-hour course *The Body Politic, Social and Environmental Justice, Art, Activism* which ran six times between 2004 and 2009 attracted people from a range of backgrounds and interests, providing them with a reflective space to connect up, inform each other, tease out issues and practices, and energise new collaborations. Our new course for young people *Shake! Young voices in arts, media, race & power* is taking this approach to 16-25 year olds.

What these all have in common is a consensus-based approach, valuing equality of process, and equality of voice. The politics of horizontalism confronts power hierarchies, and thus also confronts accepted canons of knowledge and challenges disciplinary territorialism. Research and sharing skills becomes sexy, exciting and political, and inseparable from imaginative strategy. It is a stimulus for clever targeted actions, stronger communities, arresting art interventions, and sleek data visualisations. These kinds of interdisciplinarity mean that larger and sometimes unlikely coalitions can work together, seeking common territory, each bringing to the joint cause their own motivations, their own expertise in a culture of respect.

It's the morning of Saturday 23rd January 2010. The first day of a workshop, Disobedience Makes History: Exploring creative resistance at the boundaries between art and life, *led by the Labofii at the invitation of Tate Modern. Unwittingly, Tate has planted a bomb that's about to explode in its face. John Jordan of Labofii describes in* On refusing to pretend to do politics in a museum:

> *After several months of planning, we received an email from the curators that casually ended with the paragraph: "Ultimately, it is also important to be aware that we cannot host any activism directed against Tate and its sponsors, however we very much welcome and encourage a debate and reflection on the relationship between art and activism".*[9]

The Carbon Web

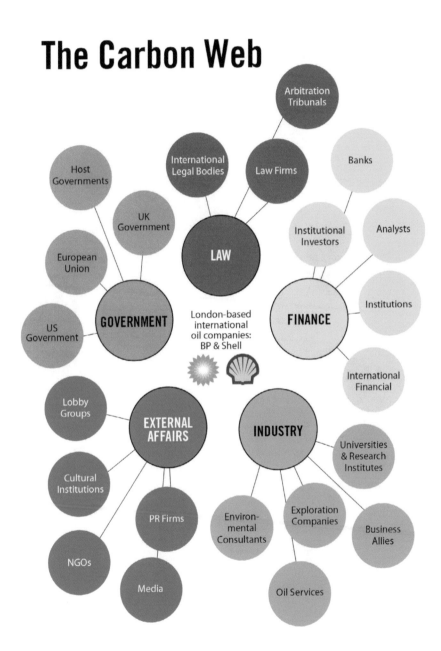

Carbon Web diagram design by Owen Bryant

The Carbon Web

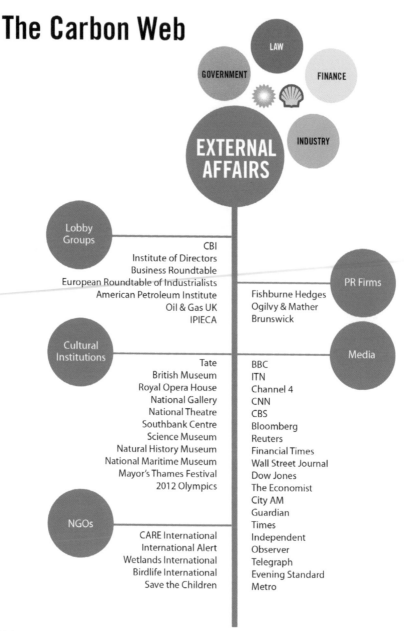

Carbon Web diagram design by Owen Bryant

Labofii decide that sharing this email is the only possible starting point for the two-day over-subscribed workshops. In an airy room at the top of Tate Modern, with panoramic views over the City, the fuse was lit. A key initial tool was the Carbon Web *– an in-depth data visualisation model developed by Platform which shows, among many things, how cultural sponsorship sits fair and square within oil companies' External Relations strategies. Such sponsorship serves a PR function: the 'feel good' factor cultivates the company's 'social licence to operate'. The more controversial the business practice, the more important it is for the company to construct and maintain this social legitimacy through careful brand strategies – which include sponsorship of the arts, sports etc.*

Through a consensus-based process with workshop participants, a new collective of artist-activists self-organises called Liberate Tate, dedicated to 'taking creative disobedience against Tate until it drops its oil company funding'.[10] Several high profile performance-interventions were planned and executed in Tates Britain and Modern. After the news broke of the catastrophic BP Deepwater Horizon blowout on 20th April 2010 in the Gulf of Mexico, Liberate Tate's well-crafted and media savvy tactics took the issue to a whole new level. On 28th June, Tate Britain held its annual Summer Party which was also celebrating 20 years of BP sponsorship. Liberate Tate performed its iconic Licence to Spill *piece at the main entrance to the party. This action received international media attention and spectacularly blasted the controversy out into the mainstream.[11] Asked to comment, Nicholas Serota, Director of Tate tellingly said '...you don't abandon friends because they have what you consider to be a temporary difficulty.'[12]*

In other words, in a tight corner, BP needs Tate, not Tate needs BP.

The Disobedience Makes History workshop facilitators projected Tate's email big on the wall, using it as a catalyst. It created outrage among the workshop group, an outrage that was harnessed by the subsequent presentation of Platform's research into how Tate sits within BP's PR universe. The *Carbon Web* has time and again provoked revelation in groupings ranging from business people who have told us that they had never before seen their work in context, to arts audiences who have not previously connected the oil industry to the cultural sector, to activists hungry for a systemic understanding of the problem and for more targets to focus on.

Platform places research at the centre of the practice, publishing many reports that lay out in detail the economic and political power structures behind the issues at hand.[13] Most of those reports are aimed at 'special publics' such as financial journalists, oil analysts, environmental NGOs, cultural sector, activists and government policy-makers. Once the research is done however, the material becomes sculptural – it can be molded and formed, worked into, in a number of different media. Or perhaps, better, it becomes like a set of moves, that can be choreographed for a number of different dance pieces for different contexts. We had been regularly supplying activists with this research, working closely with the pioneering activist group Art Not Oil,[14] for example. By the time Platform came to target oil sponsorship of the arts using the political moment of the Deepwater disaster, there was enormous fluency in the arguments, painstakingly built up over many years. By thinking about the *Carbon Web* in relation to the art world, and through networking and information-sharing with people working in the arts, we could quickly create a calm, authoritative critique, a critique which is not so easily dismissible by detractors, a rolling critique which remains supple and sustaining and over a long campaign.

In 2012, London's cultural scene is still awash with oil company sponsorship. Shell continues to find favour with Southbank Centre, National Theatre, Mayor's Thames Festival, National Maritime Museum and National Gallery. BP's logo emblazons billboards and TV ads for the 2012 Olympic Games, and in December 2011, Tate, National Portrait Gallery and the Royal Opera House announced that a five year renewal of sponsorship totalling £10 million had been agreed with BP. For now, such sponsorship continues to endorse oil consumption, to drive climate change, environmental risk, and resource inequity and sits contradictorily with Tate and others' pledges to emissions reductions through the 10:10 campaign.[15] Yet the situation is no longer a given. The £10 million deal was announced in a furore of media interest, stoked by activism, not least an 8000-strong petition submitted to Tate from Tate membership, Greenpeace supporters, Tate visitors and general public.[16] The 'social licence to operate' has been loudly critiqued, as is acutely summarised in the publication *Not If But When, Culture Beyond Oil*.[17] Moreover, in the current world of an ideological siege on state funding of the arts and in light of Arts Council England's 2011 announcement of new strategic funds to encourage corporate philanthropy, this campaign could not be more timely. Ethics, aesthetics and corporate sponsorship is the big new agenda.[18]

The Carbon Web

EXTERNAL AFFAIRS

Cultural Institutions

BP and Shell's sponsorship in London, as of 2011

BP

Shell

Tate

British Museum

National Portrait Gallery

Royal Opera House

2012 Cultural Olympiad

Science Museum

Natural History Museum

National Maritime Museum

National Gallery

National Theatre

Southbank Centre

Mayor's Thames Festival

Carbon Web research by Platform, correct in 2011.

Carbon Web diagram design by Owen Bryant

In 2002, Chin-tao Wu concluded her influential book *Privatising Culture, Corporate Art Intervention since the 1980s* with the words 'the current privileged position of corporations in the art world is not a permanent fixture'... 'it may well be that one day sites of resistance will form to question and challenge what for the present remains the dominant order.'[19] In 2008, we concluded our piece for Serpentine Gallery's *Manifesto Marathon*:

> There's a time coming, and it's coming very soon now, when our hosts the Serpentine Gallery and many other cultural institutions won't feel comfortable taking money from companies that depend on fossil fuels for their core business, such as today's sponsors of this fine Pavilion, Netjets and Kuoni. It's time to get ahead of the game.[20]

The interdisciplinary coalition of affected communities, environmentalists, artists, activists, and concerned citizens means that this particular game is definitely now on.

This chapter was written in 2012.

[1] J. Marriott and M. Minio, *The Oil Road*, Verso, London and New York, 2012

[2] B. Bernstein, *Pedagogy, Symbolic Control, and Identity: Theory, Research, Critique*, Taylor & Francis, London, 1996

[3] J. Trowell, 'Collaborative liberatory practices for global citizenship', in *Understanding Art Education, Engaging Reflexively with Practice*, N. Addison, L. Burgess, J. Steers, J.Trowell, Routledge, London, 2011, pp 134-147.

[4] Bernstein, p. 25.

[5] <http://www.no-tar-sands.org/2011/07/reverend-billy-leads-mass-exorcism-in-tate-modern-turbine-hall-over-'taint'-of-bp-sponsorship/>

[6] <http://www.guardian.co.uk/environment/blog/2011/jul/19/reverend-billy-tate-modern-bp>

[7] <http://www.youandifilms.com/2011/07/exorcism/>

[8] <http://labofii.net/>

<http://www.corporatewatch.org.uk/>

[9] <http://www.artmonthly.co.uk/magazine/site/article/on-refusing-to-pretend-to-do-politics-in-a-museum-by-john-jordan-2010/>

[10] <http://liberatetate.wordpress.com/>

[11] Over 50 pieces of press coverage were generated by this action, including a piece on Channel 4 news. Sample:

<http://www.guardian.co.uk/culture/2010/jul/02/bp-arts-sponsorship-tate-protests>

<http://www.bbc.co.uk/blogs/thereporters/willgompertz/2010/06/what_should_arts_instutions.html>

<http://www.marketingweek.co.uk/sectors/utilities/bps-sponsorship-of-the-arts-comes-under-attack/3015159.article>

[12] <http://www.thejc.com/arts/arts-interviews/34470/interview-sir-nicholas-serota>

[13] <http://issuu.com/platform-london>

[14] <http://www.artnotoil.org.uk/>

[15] <http://www.1010global.org/uk>

[16] <http://www.guardian.co.uk/artanddesign/2011/dec/13/tate-bp-partnership-environmental-protests>

[17] <Platform, Liberate Tate, Art Not Oil (November 2011) http://issuu.com/mellv/docs/cbo>

[18] <http://www.artscouncil.org.uk/funding/catalyst-arts>

[19] Chin-tao Wu, *Privatising Culture, Corporate Art Intervention since the 1980s*, Verso, London and New York, 2002 p. 304.

[20] J. Peyton Jones, H. Obrist, M. Puchner, M. Gronlund, *Serpentine Gallery Manifesto Marathon*, Koenig Books, 2009, p. 173.

N.B. All websites viewed on 29 July 2011

Engaging Ethics, Interrupting Neoliberalism: Value in Interdisciplinary Arts Practices

— Victor Jeleniewski Seidler

Engaging Across Boundaries

As a person with long academic involvement in social theory
and philosophy it is difficult to acknowledge how artistic
movements have shaped my thinking and feeling over time.
There were attempts – particularly in Marxist traditions of
aesthetics – to frame works of art in social and historical context
as expressions of their conditions of production. In a different
vein, psychoanalytically informed writings on art practice sought
to make connections with the psychic histories of artists. These
traditions when not reductive helped raise questions and open
dialogues with art practitioners not only about influences that
shaped their work but more widely about meanings that their art
might carry into the present.

Recently, especially in conceptual art practices, a different
kind of engagement emerged with art practitioners seeking to
make interventions in social and political processes as part of
an urgent ethical response to the world. They sought to engage
directly with complex social and cultural concerns, questioning
how dominant global capitalist culture has represented these
issues. There has been enormous value in interdisciplinary
engagements between social theorists and art practitioners but
the best is possibly yet to come; relatively recently a dialogue
has opened up, partly stimulated by a revival of student and
worker movements across Europe in the face of the global
financial crisis between different generations of activists. Keen
to question prevailing representations of gender, race, sexualities
and corporate power they have rediscovered that aesthetics and
politics could not be separated from each other but are entangled
within diverse relationships of power.

It was a potential strength of the critiques of knowledge that
developed in the social movements emerging from the 1970s that

challenged disciplinary boundaries and the ways in which people had become identified with their disciplinary discourses. These critiques are returning with the Occupy movements encouraging social researchers and arts practitioners to frame projects using diverse media to question the traditional consumerist logics of new globalised capitalisms.[1]

For interdisciplinary experiments to flourish you are not just looking for things that you can already make sense of within your own disciplinary logics because this means dialogue tacitly becomes a form of asset stripping. There is often little real acknowledgement that for a dialogue *to work* more is called for than some sense of mutuality or a desire to co-operate across disciplinary boundaries. There has to be openness to risk and to *feelings of trust*; toleration of spaces, gaps and silences where you do not know what to say and your discipline somehow leaves you on your own, exposed and vulnerable.

Explorations

In the exhibition *We Need to Talk about the Future* held at ICIA at the University of Bath (13 October – 17 December, 2010) Ruth Maclennan's video installations explore how individuals react to pressures of social, political and technological change and how they negotiate through these changing conditions but are also caught by them. The exhibition brought together her different *Dialogues* produced, along with other work, over a decade that reflects the tensions and intensities of corporate new capitalism and ways that it has colonised different spheres of life and framed a language that people feel bound to in ways that they often cannot really understand themselves. The neo-liberal terms of new capitalism frame a language of energy, creativity, resilience, innovation that has been traditionally associated with creative art practices. They have adopted a language that draws upon diverse sources but which imposes itself as a form that can feel inescapable. It helps to shape a particular form of experience that can feel both 'in control' because of the deployment of corporate language while at the same time stifling the very creativity and freedom that it talks about.[2]

As a social theorist who had researched relationships between masculinities, power and language I was excited to be invited to work with Maclennan in a discussion at Bath and later to write about her work to blend our explorations, not through seeking some common ground but through helping to deepen an analysis of the power of corporate language and the ways it has moved across genders within a corporate culture. Maclennan explores the dynamics and exercise of power and submission that are at work within corporate language. Even though hierarchies are not so sharp there is a pervasive system of line management that means people are accountable to line managers while seeking to avoid responsibility for making decisions. There is a constant displacement of responsibility carried in the language that is part of the *work* that language is expected to do. This becomes clear in *Dialogue #3 That's not for me to say,* Maclennan's art work triggered by a visit to the Director's dining room at the London School of Economics.[3] This enclosed room with no windows and wooden panelling suggested to the artist a depiction of a man alone, talking to camera, rehearsing his lines in preparation for speaking to colleagues. It was an educational space that had been increasingly corporatised. It was the resignation of Howard Davis as Director of the LSE because of the financial arrangements the LSE under his leadership had made with the Gadaffi family in Libya that brought the corporatisation of higher education into crisis.

Maclennan's *Dialogue* reflects the corporate character of higher education as demonstrated by the relationship between the LSE and the financial centre of the City of London. With its elite students from around the globe paying high fees, the LSE brand symbolises globalised corporate education offering a means of gaining access and status within the financial and corporate sectors. In this way knowledge has become commodified. Paulo Freire's notion of 'banking education' as a commodity passed between teacher and pupils assumed a new meaning from the 1990s with so many students competing for jobs in the financial sector.[4] The university was to be reorganised as a global corporate brand in which students become consumers of a high quality product delivered at a globally competitive price. Universities are no longer so concerned with critical engagement with society but have become businesses to provide qualifications for global educational elites.

Maclennan describes *Dialogue #3*: "it depicts an enclosed but unstable world, exposing desires suppressed in the faceless corporate business world." Acknowledging how many of the features of the corporate world have "found their way into numerous other walks of life" she suggests narrative progression somehow

Section Three — Ethics, Interdisciplinary Arts Practice and the Politics of Negotiation

Dialogue #3 (That's not for me to say)
2002, single channel video, projection/monitor, 11minutes 58 seconds

Dialogue #3 (That's not for me to say)
2002, single channel video, projection/monitor, 11minutes 58 seconds

Dialogue #3 (That's not for me to say)
2002, single channel video, projection/monitor, 11minutes 58 seconds

Dialogue #3 (That's not for me to say)
2002, single channel video, projection/monitor,
11minutes 58 seconds

"prevented from unfolding." Her work echoes Beckett, courtroom drama, corporate training videos and artists' video loops. As she describes, the work "enacts the gap between meaning and image, between the symbolic 'character' (a cipher) and the performance that he or she is caught up in." It is significant that later *Dialogues* feature men talking directly to camera and audience, enacting anxieties, fears and pleasures of a corporate masculinity somehow *tied* into expressing itself through particular language.

We witness a rehearsal of a corporate executive exploring the right intonation. He is constantly rehearsing the same lines directed towards us as audience — *rehearsing* and *trying out* ways to say the words he has learnt. The language has a life of its own illuminating a post-structuralism that suggests identities are articulated and brought into existence through language. This is why Maclennan talks about a 'character' as 'cipher' who is *spoken through* and thereby *brought into existence* through language. This challenges notions that individuals express themselves and so shape their experience through language. Rather it signals a post-structuralism that often fails to acknowledge a tension between language and experience — a tension that resonates across the boundaries of Wittgenstein's later philosophical writings and feminism in its appreciation of tension between language, power and experience — assuming that there is no experience that exists prior to language but that 'experience' is articulated and brought into existence through language.[5]

At one point in *Dialogue #3*, a tear forms in actor Ian Kelly's eye. This suggests complex interplay between language that can seem still and automatic even as it is rehearsed and the different levels of experience that it can unwittingly bring forward. We know we are witnessing an actor but at the same time recognise that corporate executives will often be *caught up* in the roles they are playing in the firm. We experience tensions as different options are rehearsed and find ourselves *switching* between experiencing ourselves as audience being addressed and identifying with the executive *struggling* with his lines. Sometimes we want him to *break out* and find other words and sentences and so escape the constraints of the language he has been given. We want him to find new lines.

Dialogues

Ruth Maclennan as an art practitioner and myself as social theorist recognised it would *take time* to think across disciplinary boundaries of art practice and social and cultural theory. At the opening of her exhibition, we created a space for dialogue where others could participate. Starting with the question – 'Are you committed to success?' we asked people to spend time in discussion with a fellow participant exploring who might have said this to them and what kind of voice of authority it could have represented? Is this a voice we might discover working inside us? How might we have *prepared* to say this to someone and could we identify with the rehearsals that had been re-enacted in the *Dialogues*? What kind of process would we have gone through to not only find the *right words* but to say them in the *right way*? For some people this seemed to bring up issues of *control* and the ways that, particularly men, might learn to use language as a means of sustaining control. But living in a post-feminist culture of greater gender equality both genders identified with these sentiments while recognising they might need *time for rehearsal* so that when they said it to someone, they were able to say it in the right way. Participants recognised issues of *timing* and different pressures in a period of financial crisis when other work is scarce. These 'messages' came to have altered meaning: people recognised that 'you might be committed to success' but if there are no jobs around, a tone of absurdity emerges.

I recalled teaching third year students in the department of Sociology at Goldsmiths who in 2008 were suddenly confronted with the realisation that the world around them *had changed* and it dawned on them, slowly at first, that their futures were not going to be as expected and they were no longer able to assume they would get well-payed jobs to quickly pay off student loans. The *future* suddenly became unsettled and de-stabilised. They had to think quite differently about the labour market and their own possible futures. They were anxious and concerned.

Sometimes it takes more time to find your way to speak about issues and you feel yourself circling around, trying to find a point of entrance that can also put you *in contact* and so in communication with the person to whom you are talking. How a dialogue is going, can show itself in body language as people move towards each other feeling for connections through dialogue, while at other times it might feel just too difficult to

Dialogue #5 (It's not your problem)
2009 single channel video, projection, 19 minutes 18 seconds

get through and *make contact.* Rather people can feel a sense of silent desperation as if they are suspended in different worlds that do not seem able to really touch each other — a lot of words are spoken but very little is understood even though people seem to be reaching out towards each other.

Maclennan's various *Dialogues* show how corporate culture can be infantilising in ways that people are obliged to articulate their experience, making them wary about thinking for themselves. They are constrained by a language that states their experience and identities for them — the language *speaks them* in ways that resonate with a post-structuralism that questions whether people can express themselves through language, without recognising how this becomes a feature of the oppressive character of corporate culture. However, they can still explore the intonations with which language can be delivered and the different connotations language carries. People in job interviews know what they are expected to say and the kind of motivation they are supposed to deliver if they want to have a chance for employment. They must show a willingness to shape their experience but also their personalities so that they *fit* the market.

Crisis

Often there is a tension between physical spaces that people find themselves in and the nature of dialogue. The wooden panelling of the Director's dining room at the LSE with its absence of light and air suggests a possible progression that is somehow prevented from unfolding. There is a kind of silent desperation as different lines are rehearsed, giving a particular edge to the crisis in higher education with the withdrawal of state funding from humanities and social sciences. Somehow this reflects the corporatization of Universities. It is as if the university has been emptied out of its understanding of education as a human value for social good and reframed as a matter of individual self-enhancement where education is a commodity. The LSE MA is priced beyond the means of most students.

The placing of dialogue in this particular setting carries an edge and inner desperation that shows momentarily in a tear, a crisis often silently carried when people sense they no longer believe in anything having sacrificed whatever beliefs and values they shared as students to the end of individual advancement and corporate profit. A climate that encouraged living 'in the fast lane' earning as much as possible through risk-taking in the present because the future is not assured. Working long hours, tied into an office culture shaped around ideas that 'greed is good' as long as you balance it with a level of 'social responsibility'.[6]

Sometimes the destroyed locations chosen by Maclennan embody her characters' inner uncertainties and silent desperation. We can read the protagonists' psychic states through the spaces in which they speak. Some rooms are empty, in the process of reconstruction. These buildings seem haunted by ghosts of the past and their working lives. The words spoken within her art work and the determination with which her protagonists pace the corridors are out of joint with their surroundings. A disjunction exists that adds to the tension of some dialogues where it sometimes feels like there is *nowhere to go* and *nothing to develop*.

Ruined spaces are often ignored by a speaker as if oblivious to their surroundings but somehow it makes a difference to *how* we hear them and our sense of what is going on at different levels of their experience.

In *Dialogue #5 (It's not your problem)*, the tension between voice and surroundings and the pacing across both inner and outer spaces reaches a particular intensity.[7] We witness a man who no longer copes with the expectations and routines of corporate culture even though he still tries. In conversation about the *Dialogue* and what motivated her to make it, Maclennan describes time as subjectively perceived so that you do not know, and she does not know as the filmmaker if this is "one moment stretched over 25 minutes or is he there for days?" Timing is stretched in different ways in different *Dialogues* but here it is stretched to breaking point reflecting both an inner crisis but also the larger global financial crisis triggered with the collapse of Lehman Brothers in 2008, as we watched the 'unlucky ones' carrying possessions away in cardboard boxes from the investment bank, hit with the crash. It was the luck of the draw.

Richard Sennett in *The Corrosion Of Character* identifies these transformed temporalities in relation to IBM. He explores how young men and women are expected to live mobile lives ready to move at any moment to a different job in a different location. But he also explores the encouragement to hold their beliefs and values lightly, ready to sacrifice anything that might get in the way of achieving promotion. They must be ready to submit and prove their willingness to do 'whatever it takes' to succeed in the corporation for 'the name of the game'. The goal is to 'get on' and

Engaging Ethics, Interrupting Neoliberalism: Value in Interdisciplinary Arts Practices — Victor Jeleniewski Seidler

Dialogue #5 (It's not your problem)
2009 single channel video, projection, 19 minutes 18 seconds

the fear is of being shown up as a 'loser' who did not 'make it'.

Few people can 'make it' — most people will fall by the way or not succeed in their ambitions. For years until the crisis hit, people were so used to living on high levels of credit with the assumption that the 'good times' would go on forever. But at the same time there was an anxiety that you could never tell what the future would bring.

Others do not know the anxieties and fears you are carrying even if they are sitting next to you. There is an inner tightness of masculinity that learns to show itself 'in control' and 'at ease' on the surface — a demonstration of how these corporate masculinities are performative. It is a matter of doing what is expected, shaping your language, experience and aspirations accordingly. Even those closest are often kept in the dark and have little idea of what is going on until it is too late. This is often the case for families in which suicide happens. Within a neo-liberal culture there is an individualisation of experience where men — and women — can feel caught within a corporate world from which others feel excluded.[8]

Explaining the thinking that went into *Dialogue #5*, Maclennan says,

> I was thinking of Icarus dropping out of the sky, unnoticed by anyone — in particular his image in the Breughel painting. Someone's trauma is happening right next to us and we aren't aware, and even if we did know, we still probably wouldn't be able to do anything about it. The feeling of the helpless witness to a crisis is important.[9]

She notes that the "personal experience of this (is) also expanded to a world-wide context" and so to financial, ecological, social and political crises. There is also "something about the character being trapped inside and suddenly bursting out. He can't be contained."[10] This is mirrored in the conditions of the natural world which cannot be completely controlled and silenced but will find ways to the surface, as do plants growing through cracks in a balcony.

Maclennan notes that within the artwork a shift is marked — moving "From repeated borrowed sentences to a stream of associative images, a monologue, or rather dialogue with himself." In some ways he is addressing himself and engaging with an inheritance of corporate language that he is pushing to its limits and through them in crisis to something else. Apropos the global financial and ecological crisis Ruth Maclennan states:

> I felt a very strong feeling of anger — directed in many
> directions, but perhaps unfocussed because how do you deal
> with anger at ideology, not at an individual — at the time
> of the so-called crisis. I felt I needed to think about what
> 'crisis' meant or might mean. A way of understanding it was
> to revisit a form, the dialogue, to explore how a crisis might
> be a means of waking up the character, of bringing him into
> the moment, and making him challenge the words he was
> hearing and repeating.[11]

As Maclennan shows a man cracking up in front of our eyes, we are witnessing scenes that make us feel uneasy for we do not like to be reminded of human vulnerability. What is shown is also the cracking up of a system at a time of global financial crisis. Might he be driven to suicide? But the fact that he is alone also reminds us that others are not seeing what is happening and that somehow we have been positioned as witnesses of a personal crisis that tells us more about the larger crisis within the public sphere.

There seems too few spaces of refuge and little vision of how life could be different and societies organised on a different basis, more in touch with people's needs. Rather than looking into a corporate world that is strange to people not working in it, we become aware of how social relations have become instrumentalised and the social world corporatised. This shows itself in the smooth surface we learn to present to others and the limited inner space we have in ourselves through which a different relationship to self and other can be created. We recognise how we have ourselves become adaptive and dissociated from ourselves.

By suggesting the possibility of different perspectives we can be encouraged to shape other contemporary imaginations to form a new relationship between public and private spheres while understanding the value of different relationships to the natural world and eco-structure. Through interdisciplinary dialogues we can hope to think across boundaries of traditional disciplines to create new political imaginations that can disrupt neo-liberal governmentalities and suggest different ways of living together on an endangered and vulnerable planet. Inequalities between the global north and south can then be addressed and people can learn to accept moral responsibility for the equal worth of all human lives and respect for nature with which we remain inextricably interconnected.

Section Three — Ethics, Interdisciplinary Arts Practice and the Politics of Negotiation

[1] For some interesting reflections upon the changing nature of globalised new capitalism and its impacts upon the formation of character in an age of intensive inequalities legitimated through the logics of neoliberalism see R. Sennett, *The Corrosion of Character: The Personal Consequences of Work in the New Capitalism*, W.W.Norton, New York, 1998 and his later book *Respect: The Formation of Character in an Age of Inequality*, Penguin Books, London, 2004.

[2] For some helpful reflections upon the nature of risk within globalised new capitalism see, for instance U. Beck, *The Risk Society: Towards a New Modernity*, Sage, London, 1992 and his *The Brave New World of Work*, Polity Press, Cambridge, 2000. For a theoretical grasp of theories of reflexive modernisation that informs Beck's work see U.Beck, A.Giddens & S. Lash, (eds), *Reflexive Modernisation*, Polity Press, Cambridge, 1995.

[3] This work was made at the London School of Economics, while Ruth Maclennan was Leverhulme Artist in Residence in the Archives at LSE.

[4] Paulo Freire's work on the commodification of knowledge and how it has helped organise particular forms of education has achieved a new relevance within neo-liberal visions. See for instance, P. Freire, *The Pedagogy of the Oppressed*, Penguin Books, Harmondsworth, 1971.

[5] For some background to Wittgenstein's later work and how it resonates in vital ways with certain forms of feminist theory see the discussion in V. J. Seidler, *Unreasonable Men: Masculinity and Social Theory*, Routledge, London and New York, 1993.

[6] For some reflections upon the changing nature of masculinities and how they are entangled with corporate culture see discussions in my *Transforming Masculinities: Men, Cultures, Bodies, Power, Sex and Love*, Routledge, London and New York, 2005.

[7] This work was made for Archway Polytechnic, Maclennan's collaborative, event-based art project that was based in Archway between 2007-2011, in association with AIR at Central Saint Martins College of Art and Design. Archway Polytechnic was supported by Cocheme Foundation, and Arts Council England. *Dialogue #5 (It's not your problem)* is distributed by LUX along with other single channel works by Maclennan. <http://lux.org.uk/collection/artists/ruth-maclennan>

[8] For helpful discussion on the nature of neoliberal ethics and the ways that it silences different voices see, for instance, N. Couldry, *Why Voices Matter: Culture and Politics after Neoliberalism*, Sage, London, 2008. For an appreciation of the role of the mass media in shaping events see D. Dagan & E. Katz, *Media Events: The Live Broadcasting of History*, Harvard University Press, Cambridge Mass, 1992 and A. Hepp and F. Krotz, (eds), *Media Events in a Global Age*, Routledge, London, 2010.

[9] R Maclennan, Personal email, 18 November, 2010. I wish to show my appreciation for the help and encouragement that Ruth Maclennan gave me to freely respond to her work and to think through some of my responses — though it was only over a couple of days our conversations reached a level of genuine dialogue as we talked about her work and she shared some of the ideas that went into their creation. She had read widely about corporate culture and this helped shape the dialogues so there were different processes of interdisciplinarity *already* going on before we even started our conversations. We were both interested in the rigidities and unspeakable violences of corporate culture and were seeking different ways to make them transparent.

[10] Maclennan, 2010.

[11] Maclennan, 2010.

Afterword

— Jane Calow

There are certain threads that run across, through and between the texts that make up this volume, creating moments and sites of rapport and resonance.

Many of the authors make reference to landscapes; those that exist in material terms, as well as imagined, psychic and metaphorical landscapes. Stratagems for travelling are suggested by different manoeuvres in spatialisation. Both Jane Rendell and Jane Trowell suggest the horizontal nature of manoeuvres in interdisciplinarity – all suggest mobility.

Ever present is identity and the corporeal body; physicality and internality, sitting alongside the play of language in the construction of subjectivities.

Other preoccupations within the texts are those of the global pressures brought to bear upon forms of representation via corporate capitalism and its influence upon and within cultural and educational institutions. Influences that have political as well as economic implications for the whole of lived, social process.

Finally, drawing to a close with notes of optimism – many contributors have signalled the transformational latency implicit within interdisciplinarity. In the concluding passage of his text, Victor Jeleniewski Seidler suggests how by thinking across boundaries, through interdisciplinary dialogue new political imaginations can be created that disrupt neo-liberal governmentalities, suggesting different ways of living together.

Interdisciplinarity resonates with the words of Richard Sennett:

Today, the crossed effect of desires for reassuring solidarity amid economic insecurity is to render life brutally simple: us-against-them coupled with you-are-on-your-own. But I'd insist that we dwell in the condition of 'not yet'.[1]

[1] R.Sennett, *Together: The Rituals, Pleasures and Politics of Cooperation*, Yale University Press, New Haven and London, 2012, p. 280.

Contributors

Brave New Alps

Bianca Elzenbaumer and Fabio Franz have collaborated under
the collective name Brave New Alps since 2005. Whilst studying
an MA in Communication Design at the Royal College of Art
they initiated the development of Department 21. Having studied
together at the Faculty of Design and Art of the Free University
of Bozen-Bolzano in Italy, their projects focus on an embedded
response to the surrounding environment, discourse and
structures of engagement they find themselves working within. In
2007, Bianca gained a Postgraduate Certificate in International
Peacekeeping and Conflict Mediation from the Faculty of
Educational Science of the University of Bologna employing this
knowledge in the development of their interdisciplinary practice.
Brave New Alps are currently working on the research project
Designing Economic Cultures, which is related to Bianca's Ph.D.
at the Design Department of Goldsmiths, University of London.

Dr Carol Brown

Carol Brown's dance practice takes place at the intersections between movement, architecture, new media and music; it includes solos, group works for theatre, performance installations and site responsive works. As Artist in Residence at the Place Theatre London she founded Carol Brown Dances together with sound artist Russell Scoones. The company has been a vehicle for their continued collaboration presenting work at numerous festivals including Roma Europa, Dance Umbrella, 4+4 Days in Motion, Sobre Saltos, Dies de Danca, Prague Quadrenniale, British Dance Edition and the New Zealand International Festival of the Arts. Brown is an Associate Professor at the University of Auckland where she has developed *Choreographic Research Aotearoa* a locus for experimental performance and connecting conversations. Through MAP Movement Architecture Performance, Brown and Scoones have created numerous site responsive works with performance designer Dorita Hannah including *Mnemosyne* (Prague Quadrenniale 2011), *Tongues of Stone* (Perth 2011) and *1000 Lovers* (Auckland Arts Festival White Night 2013). Brown is the recipient of a number of awards including the Jerwood Award, NESTA Dream Time and in 2003 the Ludwig Forum International Prize for Innovation. She is a Visiting Reader in Choreography at Roehampton University, London.

Dr Jane Calow

Jane Calow is an artist and writer who has exhibited widely. Performed nationally and internationally, her artwork *Traject* explored the idea of a 'moveable site', highlighting themes of physical and psychic spatialisation informed by the psychoanalytical structure of trauma. Her artist's book produced as part of *Traject* is held in Tate Britain library archive. Jane directed the international interdisciplinary conference *Public Representation and Private Mourning: Commemoration and Memorial* (UWE, 2002). She is currently working on an artwork developed from *Traject* entitled *Mantle*, working with mourning and grief. She published as Guest Editor on the 12th edition of the Routledge journal Mortality, entitled *Memoria, Memory, and Commemoration* and has lectured at the University of Bath on the MSc in Death and Society. She co-directed the international symposium *Present: trauma/art/representation* at ICIA (2006).

Jane has also worked as a curatorial consultant to ICIA on the 2009 programme theme entitled *Arts, Spatialisation and Memory* for which she co-directed an international symposium. She was Head of Fine Art as Social Practice at the University of Wolverhampton. She was also Research Fellow at the Centre for Contextual, Public and Commemorative Art at the University of the West of England.

Dr Daniel Hinchcliffe

Daniel Hinchcliffe is a curator, artist and writer. As Head of Visual Arts at the Institute of Contemporary Interdisciplinary Arts (ICIA) University of Bath he curated exhibitions, interdisciplinary residencies and projects with artists including Terry Atkinson, David Bainbridge, Bobby Baker, Ingrid Pollard, Stephen Gill, Wendy McMurdo, Chila Kumari Burman, Ruth Maclennan, Uriel Orlow, Anne Tallentire and Janek Schaefer. During this time he curated and expanded the University of Bath art collection. Daniel has also worked in numerous situations as an artist in public and community contexts. He has devised, organised and chaired many international symposia, conferences and talks. Daniel co-edited, *Advances in Art and Urban Futures Volume 2: Recoveries and Reclamations* (Bristol, Intellect Books, 2002). He has also written for the journal *Mortality* (Routledge). He taught for six years on the BA (Hons) Fine Art as Social Practice course at the University of Wolverhampton. His PhD was concerned with public art commissioning as part of urban regeneration.

Laura Mansfield

Laura Mansfield is an independent curator and writer. She works closely with other artists in the development of both publication and exhibition based projects. Recent projects include the publication series *FEAST* and the group exhibition *Cacotopia* at the International Anthony Burgess Foundation, Manchester. Laura is currently curating a two year programme of artist's film and video works as part of her online project *Pala//here is always somewhere else//*. She is a PhD candidate at MIRIAD, Manchester School of Art.

Professor Mike Pearson

Mike Pearson studied archaeology in University College, Cardiff (1968–71). He was a member of R.A.T. Theatre (1972–3) and an artistic director of Cardiff Laboratory Theatre (1973–80) and Brith Gof (1981–97). He continues to make performance as a solo artist, in collaboration with artist/designer Mike Brookes as Pearson/Brookes (1997–present) and for National Theatre Wales. He is co-author with Michael Shanks of *Theatre/Archaeology* (2001) and author of *In Comes I: Performance, Memory and Landscape* (2006), *Site-specific Performance* (2010), *Mickery Theater. An Imperfect Archaeology* (2011) and *Marking Time: performance, archaeology and the city*. He is currently Leverhulme Research Fellow and Professor of Performance Studies, Department of Theatre, Film and Television Studies, Aberystwyth University.

Professor Jane Rendell

Jane Rendell is a writer, art critic and architectural historian/ theorist/designer, whose work explores inter- and trans-disciplinary crossings between architecture, art, feminism and psychoanalysis. She has put forward concepts of 'critical spatial practice' (2002/6) and 'site-writing' (2007/10) through such authored books as *Site-Writing* (2010), *Art and Architecture* (2006), and *The Pursuit of Pleasure* (2002). She is currently working on a new book on transitional spaces in architecture and psychoanalysis. She is co-editor of *Pattern* (2007), *Critical Architecture* (2007), *Spatial Imagination* (2005), *The Unknown City* (2001), *Intersections* (2000), *Gender, Space, Architecture* (1999) and *Strangely Familiar* (1995). Recent texts have been commissioned by artists such as Jasmina Cibic, Apollonia Susteric and transparadiso, and institutions such as FRAC Centre, Orléans, and Hamburger Bahnhof, Berlin. She is on the Editorial Board for *ARQ* (Architectural Research Quarterly), *Architectural Theory Review*, *The Happy Hypocrite*, *The Issues* and the *Journal of Visual Culture in Britain*, and *Ultime Thule: Journal of Architectural Imagination*. She is Professor of Architecture and Art at the Bartlett, UCL. www.janerendell.co.uk

Professor Victor Jeleniewski Seidler

Victor Jeleniewski Seidler is Professor of Social Theory in the Department of Sociology, Goldsmiths College, University of London. He is well known for his writings on gender, particularly in relation to men and masculinities in texts such as *Rediscovering Masculinity: Reason, Language and Sexuality*; *Unreasonable Men: Masculinity and Social Theory*; *Man Enough: Embodying Masculinities*, *Transforming Masculinities* and *Young Men and Masculinities: Global Cultures and Intimate Lives*. He has written widely in areas of social and cultural theory and philosophy including the publications *Urban Fears and Global Terrors: Citizenship, Multicultures and Belongings After 7/7*, and the publication *Embodying Identities: Culture, Differences and Social Theory* (Policy Press, 2010). His most recent work is *Remembering Diana: Cultural Memory and the Reinvention of Authority* (Palgrave Macmillan, 2013) and *Remembering 9/11: Terror, Trauma and Social Theory* (Palgrave Macmillan, 2013).

Dr Becky Shaw

Becky Shaw is a visual artist and academic, making work that explores the relationship between objects and people. Since 1995 she has worked mainly to public commission, devising live, photographic, sculptural, written and print responses to large organisations including schools, universities, workplaces, public housing centres, hospitals and galleries. Examples include *Transfer* where the entire art collection of a hospital (400+ works) was moved to a small contemporary art gallery in Manchester and *Local Colour* a work that involved taking a photographic sample of every women's garment in every shop window in Preston, for three consecutive months. Current works focus on objects that move through space via production. This includes examining an 'inlaid' table at Lady Lever Art Gallery, Portsunlight, and printing a book with 70 kilo's of Texas Holey Rock, removed from terrariums at Cork Airport. A 2013/14 Cocheme Fellowship at AIR, Central St Martins is providing the time to explore concrete production at Lafarge Tarmac, Kings Cross.

Previous commissioners have included Grizedale Art, Cumbria, New Art Gallery Walsall, ICIA University of Bath, and Hayward Gallery, London. In 2002 she won the Amstelveen Art Incentive Prize. In 1998 she received a doctorate, following a lengthy collaboration with Liverpool Marie Curie Centre. Between 2000 and 2006 Shaw was co-director of Static Gallery, Liverpool. She is currently Postgraduate Research Tutor for the Art and Design Research Centre at Sheffield Institute of Arts, Sheffield Hallam University.

Jane Trowell

Jane Trowell is an educationalist and artist who has worked with Platform since 1991. Jane concentrates on pedagogical and social process aspects of Platform's work. In her own right, she has worked in contemporary galleries and community theatre, worked in teacher education in art and design, as well as teaching Critical Studies and Art History at Secondary, Further and Higher Education levels investigating methods of radical education for social justice.